RAM

after sita's departure

Dr. Ashok Sharma

M.Sc., Proficiency in French,

Ph.D.(Maths)

REDGRAB books

redgrabbooks.com

Published By

Redgrab Books Pvt. Ltd.

942, Mutthiganj, Prayagraj, 211003

www.redgrabbooks.com

contact@redgrabbooks.com

Price in india : 250/- INR

First published by Redgrab Books in 2025

Printed and bound in India

Cover Design & Typesetting by Redgrab Books team

ISBN : 978-81-19562-80-0

Dedication

Mother: Late Siya Rani Sharma

Father: Late Prem Shankar Sharma

Preface

Meditation, worship, chanting of mantras or reading of holy scriptures are our attempts to communicate with God.

His experience is beyond words and his blessings evoke a feeling of gratitude. Every attempt to deny him is proof of his existence. Attempts to deny him can also be attempts to avoid him.

Does anyone have a scale to measure the appropriateness of his actions? His journey in the human body took place in several stages?

Thanks to him even for the darkness, otherwise how would we have come to know the light. The life journeys of Ram and Krishna were also a part of this journey. Those who have made up their mind to question and ridicule the Indian cultural heritage, are naturally doomed to keep questioning the symbols of Indian identity, Ram and Krishna, and to keep throwing mud on them with the help of various imaginary incidents, making them a symbol of so-called modernity and secularism.

Frequently, they disregard established facts, labeling them as mere fiction, yet their perspective shifts dramtically when it comes to other faiths.

It is important to note that there was a time when a single physician was responsible for treating all ailments; however, with advancements in medical science, we now have specialists for various bodily concerns. In a similar vein, Hinduism, which possesses profound spiritual wisdom, has sought to personify the Divine in diverse forms to address different aspects of life. Goddesses such as Saraswati represent knowledge, Lakshmi symbolizes wealth, and Durga embodies strength. Additional concepts like

Shiva pertain to the essence of Shivatva, Brahma to creation, and Vishnu to sustenance.

You see that creation was considered a task of great intelligence and thinking and Brahma was imagined to have five heads and considering upbringing to be a big task Vishnu was imagined to have four hands. The justification of Durga having eight arms, Saraswati having a Veena in her hand and Lakshmi being on a lotus etc. can also be easily understood. Different hymns and different mantras for them are also an effort in this direction.

They made their idols and their pictures. Decorated them. Offered flowers to them, performed aarti and worshipped them. Some people keep the picture of Hanuman ji or any other god or goddess in their pocket or purse because their religion allows them to worship God with a feeling of friendship and love. Have you ever seen a slave making and decorating the idol of his master or keeping his picture in his pocket with respect and love?

In Hinduism, meditation is of great importance. For those who want to make efforts in this direction, these idols or pictures often help them in their efforts. Hindus know that these idols or pictures are only a means to reach God, not God himself, otherwise they would not remove the old idols of Lakshmi-Ganesh, Durga or Ganpati and bring new idols every year.

To say that Hindus have thirty-three crore gods and goddesses is also a mockery of religion. No person can even tell the names of thirty-three gods and goddesses.

Like other religions, in Hinduism too, there is only one God or Brahma. In Sanskrit, there is a saying, "Eko Brahma, Dwitiyo Nasti". The truth is that anyone who takes support of any trunk of a very old banyan tree is taking support of that one banyan tree only. Where can there be any confusion or dispute in this?

Additionally, Dr. Ram Manohar Lohia articulated a profound

perspective "The question of whether Ram's birth is significant pales in comparison to the reality that millions find solace in his name. He becomes a companion in our joys and a source of strength in our sorrows. This sentiment holds greater value than mere historical accuracy. Lohia further remarked that Ram traversed the land from north to south, while Krishna journeyed from east to west, suggesting that their roles were to unite the nation across these dimensions.

The essence of Ram is encapsulated in his defined character, Krishna embodies a liberated spirit, and Shiva represents the infinite."

Regarding this book, I found myself pondering a suitable theme for several days. One evening, as I lay in bed reflecting on the day's events, the idea struck me: why not explore the emotional turmoil Ram must have experienced following Sita's departure? As I began to articulate Ram's mental state, I was overwhelmed by an indescribable feeling that persisted throughout the writing process, as if I simultaneously existed in that era. This sensation could be described as a stroke of good fortune.

Without going into much detail, I hope that while reading it, you too will be able to experience the essence of that time and become a part of his journey.

Gratitude is extended to Shri Shiv Narayan Mishra, a distinguished senior litterateur of Gosainganj, Lucknow

Ashok Sharma

Contents

1.
In the Memories

Although Sita was no longer present, her essence remained deeply embedded in the hearts of the people, creating an enduring legacy. The court was convened to address pressing matters. Disturbing reports from Kekay, Kaikeyi's homeland, indicated that the Gandharvas were wreaking havoc, and her brother, King Yudhajit, was struggling hard to defend his territory. The kingdom of Ayodhya was prepared to extend assistance to Kekay; however, no formal request for aid had been made thus far, leading the court to deliberate on the necessity of patience in this situation. Other matters were also presented for consideration.

In the absence of Sita, the bond between Janakpuri and Mithila had grown cold. This deterioration in relations was a topic of discussion during the meeting, which naturally included references to Ashwamedha Yagya and Sita herself.

The weight of Sita's words lingered heavily in Ram's heart. As the discussions concluded, he rose from his seat. Upon exiting, he noticed that evening had already fallen, and a sense of melancholy enveloped him. Rather than retreating to his usual quarters, he made his way to the terrace of the palace. Ram ascended the stairs.

Upon reaching the terrace, he felt the chill of the evening breeze, which was brisk and invigorating. He stood there, gazing up at the sky, as if in search of something He then turned his gaze to the direction of that spot where Sita's footprints had been discovered prior to her departure.

He lingered there for a moment, bowing his head before making his way slowly to the edge of the terrace, where numerous flower plants thrived in earthen pots. During her lifetime, Sita had nurtured these plants with great care. After she left, Ram frequently viSeeted this area, standing by the plants and admiring the flowers that blossomed within them. This brought back memories of Sita and filled him with a pleasant feeling.

On this particular day, he paused to observe the flowers for a while and then bent down to gently pluck one, cradling it delicately between his palms. He remained seated, and before long, his gaze softened, as a dream began to take shape in his mind.

This place was a little isolated from the rest of the building and after Sita left, whenever memories of Sita started to surround him, he used to come to this room in search of solitude. He played the Veena very well and he had kept his Veena in this room.

When Ram came into the room, he sat like this for some time, then got up, very carefully put the flower in his palm aside, sat near the Veena and started playing its strings. After a while he picked up the Veena, kept it in his lap and sat with his back and head against the wall. Keeping Sita in mind and holding the Veena in his hand, Ram closed his eyes and his fingers started playing on the strings of the Veena. The room seemed to be filled with divine music. He remained immersed in that music for a long time with his eyes closed.

Gradually it seemed as if his mind was getting lost somewhere. The speed of the fingers playing the Veena started slowing down, and gradually stopped. He sat like this for some time and then he did not know when he fell asleep and slowly a dream filled his eyes.

In this dream, he found himself in a stunning realm filled with trees, flowers, and birds, accompanied by enchanting fairies of vibrant colours. Among them was a golden fairy, likely their princess, adorned with a magnificent crown that sparkled with radiant gems. Their laughter filled the air as if joy was their very essence. The golden fairy stepped forward, her laughter echoing, with the other fairies following closely behind. She paused frequently by the blooming flowers, seemingly conversing with them. Each time she stopped to speak and gently caress a flower; the flower would gain an additional luster beyond its natural hue.

Suddenly a bird landed on her hand.

"What is it?" the golden fairy inquired of the bird.

"There is a new bird over there, unlike any we have ever seen," the bird replied.

"What is it like?" she asked.

"Bigger than us and..."

"And what else?"

"Very beautiful too."

"Alright, where is it? Let us go and see," said the golden fairy, and they proceeded onward. The bird led the way, followed by the golden fairy, with the other fairies trailing behind.

The newly arrived bird, perched on a tree branch, was taken aback by the sight of the approaching group. It became a little cautious and moved to fly, but the fairy princess signalled him to stop. The bird complied. The golden fairy observed that this bird was indeed larger than ordinary ones, adorned with vibrant colours and remarkable beauty.

"How did you arrive here?" inquired the angel.

"Simply by flying," replied the bird.

"From where have you come?"

"From a far off place."

"How is your homeland?"

"It is exceedingly beautiful."

"Is it more splendid than our fairy realm?"

"I cannot make that comparison, but it is certainly distinct from this."

The golden fairy felt a strong desire to witness that place and asked the bird, "Will you please guide me to that place?"

"Certainly, you please follow me," the bird responded, taking flight toward its home. The golden angel followed closely behind. After a considerable distance, the city of the bird came into view. They soared above the city for a while, and the fairy wished to explore it more intimately.

Eager to see the city more closely, the angel came down quite low, when suddenly an arrow shot by a hunter came and hit her in the chest. Pari's chest was filled with blood. She fell down screaming in pain, and it was her misfortune that there was a pile of burning sticks at the place where she fell. The bird saw this and started hovering around the angel, flapping its wings and screaming.

Ram woke up startled. What kind of dream was this? A shiver ran through his entire body. He felt as if the golden fairy was Sita and the bird was he himself, but the one who shot the arrow? Who was he?

Ram remembered those who had pointed fingers at Sita's character; a pained smile appeared on his lips. 'There is no dearth of problems in life,' he said to him-self. Some lines appeared on his forehead, perhaps Ravana was also remembered and who was Ravana?

2.
Women's Deliberations

Ashamed of his defeat, filled with remorse and grief-stricken, the demon king Sumali was sitting with some of his trusted companions near a big rock on the seashore.

Even while living here, he had not forgotten Lanka and his old glory. Once, along with his two brothers Malyavan and Mali, he had made Lanka so glorious and prosperous and there was so much gold there in that it came to be known as the Golden Lanka.

These three brothers, sons of Sukesha and Devavati, were very brave and valiant, but after Mali was killed in the Devasur war over supremacy over a gold mine located on the seashore, the defeated Sumali along with his remaining companions went to live on an island located far in the sea, but this place was also not very far from the reach of the gods. Sumali stayed there for a few days, then went to live on another island very far from there. It was very far away and surrounded by a very deep sea.

Sumali looked towards the direction of Lanka. Who knows what was going through his mind. The defeated and tormented demon king closed his eyes.

Daksh's three daughters Diti, Adit and Danu were married to sage Kashyap. Their children were called Daityas, Devas and Danavas respectively. There was no animosity between Daityas and Danavas but they often had conflicts with Aditi's sons, the gods, over social thinking and rituals as well as over wealth and the boundaries of kingdoms.

After Sumali fled from Lanka, the gods took over Lanka and handed it over to Kuber, son of Vishrava Rishi, as their representative. Vishrava, son of Pulastya Rishi, was learned, brilliant, well behaved, disinterested in pleasures and an ascetic. Kuber was his brave and valiant son. In Lanka, he got so much wealth collected by Sumali and his brothers that Kuber came to be known as the God of Wealth.

Remembering all this and his defeat, Sumali's eyes started burning with anger and shame. He could not keep his eyes closed. He opened his eyes and looked at the sea water. It was just dawn. The sun was rising above the sea and red color was scattered on the sea water. Sumali felt that this redness had filled his eyes. He looked towards his group and called out,

"Subahu."

Subahu was Sumali's most trusted person. He appeared.

"Demon lord, pease order," he said.

"Subahu, have you thought, how long will we continue to live like fugitives after losing our empire and Kuber will continue to rule there."

"O demon king, Kuber is very powerful and brilliant."

"Do we demons lack valour and brilliance, Subahu?"

"No, but there is something special about Kuber."

"What are you hinting at, Subahu, why don't you say it clearly?"

"He is the son of Vishrava, the grandson of Prajapati Brahma and son of sage Pulastya."

The words pierced Sumali's heart.

"So…." he said. His voice had become very heavy. Subahu wanted to say that being the son of Vishrava is indeed special but he could not say so and remained silent. After being lost in thought and quiet for some time, Sumali stood up. As soon as he stood up, all the demons stood up and the meeting ended there.

By the time Sumali reached his palace, the tension on his face had eased somewhat and it appeared from his face as if he had reached a decision. Reaching the inner room of the palace, he asked a maid to call his daughter Kaikasi.

Kaikasi was busy with her daily chores at this time of the morning. She was a little surprised by her father's sudden call, but leaving her work, she appeared before her father.

"Pranam Taat (father)," Kaikasi greeted Sumali.

"Oh Kaikasi, please come on," saying this Sumali almost stood up and signaled Kaikasi to sit on the seat in front of him. This kind of welcome from her father surprised her again. She was familiar with his nature and worries. When she sat down, Sumali said,

"Kaikasi."

"Taat."

"Kaikasi, I have called you for a special consultation."

Kaikasi was surprised once again. Her father had his ministers for consultation, and till date her father had never included her in any consultation.

"Taat." Saying this Kaikasi started looking towards Sumali.

"Kaikasi, you have seen the glory of your clan in Lanka."

"Yes."

"And today you are seeing our condition as well."

"Yes."

"Kaikasi, should we not try to regain our kingdom, our glory, our Lanka by putting everything at stake? Should we accept our situation and sit quietly?"

"No, we cannot sit quietly," said Kaikasi.

"Yes Kaikasi, this is a question of the prestige of the demons."

"Yes Taat."

"What if one of us has to sacrifice something for this?" asked Sumali.

"Even the sacrifice of life has no meaning for this",

"Kaikasi, I too was expecting such an answer from you," said Sumali.

"Taat, if I have any role in re-establishing the demon clan, I will be proud of it."

With this answer of Kaikasi, Sumali became very serious and calm for a few moments, then he said,

"Kaikasi, I have a plan in my mind and your role will be the most important in it."

"Tell me quickly, I am ready."

"Kaikasi, the one who is ruling Lanka at present is Kuber, who is very powerful and brilliant. We need a warrior like him to fight Kuber."

"Yes."

"And you can give that."

Kaikasi was speechless at this statement of Sumali. She was not able to understand anything. She looked at Sumali's face. There was a very harsh expression on his face. She asked courageously,

"But how?"

"Kaikasi, the reason why Kuber is so brave and illustrious is that he is the great grandson of Prajapita Brahma and the son of Vishrava."

"Yes, Taat."

"Then you can provide me with another son of Vishrava who is not only more brave, illustrious and valiant than Kuber, but who can also fight with Kuber on behalf of us demons."

Kaikasi shuddered at the meaning of Sumali's words, but still she felt that she must have misunderstood, this cannot be the meaning of her father's words, so she gathered courage and asked,

"What do you mean?"

Sumaali looked at Kaikasi on hearing her say this. Kaikasi's expressions could be read easily on her face. Sumali's mind was disturbed for a few moments but he had already expected this kind of reaction from Kaikasi and he had come with some decision, so he strengthened his mind and said,

"You will have to get such a son from Vishrava."

Kaikasi became pale. She will have to become the wife of a person like a father. If her life was demanded, she would gladly give it, then she would not have to die every day. Kaikasi looked at Sumali, then looked at the void. It seemed from her face that she would cry any moment, but Kaikasi laughed with tears in her eyes.

Sumali knew that this proposal would hurt Kaikasi very much. He was hoping that Kaikasi would cry badly after hearing this. Sumali was ready for this, but this laughter tore him from inside. He could not sit in front of Kaikasi so he got up and went out of the room. Kaikasi saw Sumali leave, looked at the void once again and then took her clothes in both hands, put them on her face and started crying. After crying her heart out, she wiped her face and slowly walked out of the room.

Kaikasi went from there and sat in her room. She was unable to think of whom to tell her pain to. She could tell her mother, but she would hardly be able to say anything other than her father's opinion. Kaikasi remembered her friend Mani. Kaikasi was very close to her and she was also very intelligent. Kaikasi felt as if her power of thinking and understanding had ended. She asked a maid to call Mani. Mani came. Tears had dried on

Kaikasi's face. She became worried.

"What has happened?" Mani asked.

"Father had called me," Kaikasi said.

"Then."

Kaikasi narrated the entire story. Mani was stunned at the proposal of getting a son from sage Vishrava.

"Oh!" Saying this she took a deep breath and then said

"And you can't refuse it?"

Kaikasi had thought so much in the time it took for Mani to come.

"I can't," she said.

"Why?"

"It is a question of the prestige and glory of the demon clan and then the wish of the father."

"Just a wish?"

Kaikasi remained silent on this question. Mani gave a long "hmm" on her silence and then said,

"Why only you for this work?"

Even in so much sorrow Kaikasi thought of a joke,

"Will you go to that sage? Go away, I will tell your father.''

The words were said in jest, but the princess had said them, Mani trembled from head to toe, she could only say this much

"M...M...M...I'' Mani's flow of speech was broken.

"I am joking Mani, I can never let you be sacrificed.''

Mani came back to normal but the word 'sacrifice' gave her a strong shock. 'Sacrifice' - really it is a sacrifice, she thought.

"What are you thinking Mani?'' Kaikasi asked.

"Really this work is a sacrifice,'' Mani said.

"Yes, and then as big the work is, so big a sacrifice will have to be given.''

"But why only you?'' Mani asked again.

"You are right, Mani, when there are so many vergins, why only this princess? But Mani, can you answer one thing?"

"What?"

"Why not me? Where there is talk of sacrifice, why not the royal family first?"

Mani became silent in response to this question.

There was silence for some time, then Kaikasi spoke

"Mani tell me one thing."

"What?"

"I will play a major role in bringing back the prestige and glory of the demon clan, this great fortune and the great misfortune of making me the wife of a person like my father, I have to live both, should I laugh or cry?" Saying this Kaikasi laughed very sadly, shook her head and then got up and rested her head on the wall and started sobbing.

Mani came near her and started caressing her. After crying her heart out, Kaikasi raised her head, wiped her eyes with a cloth and said, "Mani, will you do one thing for me?"

"I will,"

"Then go and tell my father that I am ready to sacrifice myself."

Mani's brain was not working. Even after hearing this, she sat quietly for some time, then after a while she herself started crying.

"Don't cry, you should be happy that your friend is being useful to the demon clan," saying this Kaikasi held Mani's hand and then added,

"Yes Mani, I saw my father's eyes when he made this proposal. This was not only his wish but it also contained the order of the demon king. You will not be allowed to think of anything else except accepting this good fortune of saving the clan." Saying this Kaikasi with tearful eyes shook her head and laughed sarcastically, and went with Mani to stand at the door of Sumali's room.

Then Kaikasi held both the hands of Mani, looked at her, pressed her lips and took a deep breath. She dropped her eyelids and the teardrops got stuck between her eyelashes and then rolled down to her cheeks. Kaikasi was holding Mani's palms. She touched the back of his fingers to her eyes. Mani's fingers got wet with Kaikasi's tears.

"I am coming, don't go," said Kaikasi. With a bitter smile on her lips and tears in her eyes, she went to Sumali's room. Sumali was not inside, but Kaikasi seemed to be out of her senses. She went near Sumali's seat and said,

"I have come, Taat."

And then she stood with her head bent as if Sumali was sitting there. Just then, Sumali returned from somewhere. He saw Mani at the door of the room. Sumali knew that this daughter of one of his prominent chiefs was Kaikasi's best friend. Seeing Mani at the door of his room, he felt that she must have brought some message from Kaikasi. 'I don't know what Kaikasi must have sent me', he thought. He was not expecting any reply so soon, but what if Kaikasi refused. As soon as this thought came to his mind, his face hardened. He did not want to hear 'no'. 'Let's see what she says' he thought and looking at Mani asked,

'How come you have come Mani, do you want to say something?'

'No, I don't want to say anything, but Kaikasi is inside your room,'

Mani said.

'Okay' saying this Sumali went inside the room. Kaikasi was still standing in front of his seat with her head bowed as if she was a stone statue. Sumali looked at Kaikasi and sat on his seat. Now he looked at Kaikasi's face.

Kaikasi's face was completely expressionless. Sumali read the words written on Kaikasi's face and the pain in the father's heart for his daughter shook him, but soon the ruler inside him woke up. He strengthened himself and said,

"Do you want to say something, Kaikasi?"

"Yes." Kaikasi said.

Sumali looked at Kaikasi with questioning eyes but did not ask anything.

"Your command is paramount, father," Kaikasi stated, her voice resonating with sorrow throughout the room. Following this, Kaikasi rushed out, embraced Mani, and both began to weep.

A heart
Cried a lot
Wept tears of blood
But none was present
To see them.

Subsequently, Sumali sent Kaikasi to the ashram of Vishrava Muni. At that time, Vishrava Muni was in his middle age. Kaikasi and Vishrava were the parents of Ravan, Kumbhakarna, and Vibhishana, while Suparnakha was their daughter.

xxxxxxx

Kaikasi had been living in Vishrava Muni's ashram for many years. After Kaikasi's marriage to Vishrava Muni, Sumali had started living in Vishrava's ashram with his eleven sons with the aim of moulding Kaikasi's children according to his wishes.

Kumbhakarna, Ravana, Vibhishan and Suparnakha had all reached adolescence and were growing up playing with their uncles. Suparnakha's real name was VajRamni, but her nails were naturally long, beautiful and well-shaped, so she was also lovingly called as Suparnakha.

Among Kaikasi's sons, Kumbhakarna was very lazy and a big eater. The truth is that he only loved to eat and sleep and he used to sleep very soundly and for very long periods of time.

On the contrary, Ravana was not only very sharp, agile and quick-witted, but had also become very skilled in Yoga by learning it from his father and had kept his body very well built.

Kumbhakarna, Ravana and Suparnakha were very much under the influence of their maternal grandfather, the demon king Sumali, but Vibhishan still took after his father Vishrava and was of a Satvik nature.

Suparnakha, being the youngest and loved by all, was not only naughty and playful, but had also become very stubborn.

Meanwhile, Kaiksi's friend Mani had also got married. She used to come to her maternal home often, but as Kaiksi's father and brothers had also started living in the ashram of Muni Vishrava, hence Kaiksi mostly stayed there only. Due to this reason, Mani and Kaiksi could not meet, but once when Mani came to her parent's home, she made an effort and succeeded in coming to Vishrwa's Ashram to meet Kaikasi.

Hearing about Mani's arrival, Kaikasi almost came running to meet her and as soon as they met, both of them hugged each other.

"Mani, how are you?'' Kaiksi asked

"I am fine. Very fine and how are you?"

"Quite well and happy too." Kaikasi replied.

Mani had idea of Kaikasi's pain, so she asked again,

"Are you really happy?"

"You can see, I have become the mother of four children and to increase my prestige, my father and all eleven brothers Prahast, Akampan, Vikat etc. have also come and started living here. Now how much more happiness can I aspire for?"

Kaikasi's words had sarcasm and pain too. Mani understood her friend's mind and asked,

"There must be some reason behind your father and brother coming and living here, Kaikasi."

"Yes, one thing is that there should be no doubt in the fulfillment of the purpose for which I was sent here and this thing had to be instilled in the minds of the children from the very beginning."

"And besides this?"

"Apart from this, until the children grow up and become capable of fighting Kuber and taking back Lanka, they have to stay near Lanka and remain familiar with the conditions there and also avoid getting into trouble with the gods. For this, which place could have been more suitable than the ashram of Kuber's father."

"Hmm," Mani said, then added.

"And Rishi Vishrava."

"He is Ok," said Kaikasi in a very neutral tone.

Then after some formalities, when the friends sat together and joined their heads, Mani asked,

"How did everything happen?"

"Which thing?"

"I know that your father's men had brought and left you here, but how did you endure everything after that?"

"Is there any use in remembering those things after so many years, Mani? I have forgotten those things."

"Have you really been able to forget those things, Kaikasi?"

Kaikasi laughed painfully.

"It is difficult to forget them, but I do try to forget them."

"Then leave it."

There was an uncomfortable silence for some time, then Kaikasi said,

"Mani, people say that by telling it to someone close, lessens pains."

"So is said."

"Then listen," Kaikasi said.

"Mani, some of father's trusted people brought me from there and quietly left me here. I sat and cried for a long time at the same place where they had left me, then suddenly Vishrava himself came there.

Seeing me crying, he asked me about my introduction and the reason for crying. I had never seen him and had not heard anything about him before my father's speek about him, but from the way he spoke I understood that he must be Vishrava.''

"I am Kaikasi, daughter of demon king Sumali,'' I said,

"How did you reach here?''

"My father's people have left me here.''

"Here in my ashram, but why?''

"What could I tell Mani? How could I tell why I was left there?''

Mani could not think of any answer to this, she just put her hand on her chest and said

"Oh".

"Then what did you do?'' she asked.

"Nothing, just kept weeping.''

"Then.''

"Vishrava tried to console me saying not to weep. He aasured me to carry me safely to my father."

"Then.''

"I cannot go back there. Please take me under your protection," I said.

"What do you mean by it?" Vishrava asked.

"What does sheltering a woman mean for a man?"

"I don't think I would like to interpret what anyone else would presume listening to your words or maybe I am not able to understand the meaning of your words, but yes, you can stay here as long as you wish,"he further added.

"Mani, I started living there, but people started whispering about why a single unmarried girl is living in this ashram. Therefore, as per my father's wish, I made up my mind to request him for marrying me and one day seeing the opportunity, I said it to him-

"Rishivar, the truth is that my father wished that I should marry you and get a virtuous son. That's why he has sent me to your ashram.

Mani, I used to think that he was a Rishi, a sage, knowledgeable and wise with virtuous thoughts, he would say, You are of my daughter's age, how can I marry you? I will talk to your father to find a groom as per your wish. I would try to explain it to him, but I was surprised when he readily agreed to this marriage.

After staying in his ashram for so many days and seeing his daily routine, I had developed some respect for him in my mind, but when he readily agreed to marry a girl of his daughter's age, it ended, even though I was sent here for this very reason."

"His cosent must have caused a lot of pain."

"Yes ofcourse and the ray of hope left in my mind that may be Vishrava would save me from this injustice, died."

"And after marriage with him?''

"As soon as my father came to know about this marriage, he came and started living here with his eleven children. Mani, it is difficult to understand how low someone can go for his selfishness."

Mani could not say anything. There was an uncomfortable silence for some time and then Kaikasi said,

"Every girl gets married. I too got married and had children. All the same, yet so different."

'What kind of incidents happen in our lives? Externally similar to others but internally so different."

"Yes, and circumstances teach us to tolerate everything."

"That means there is more tolerance and less love in your life."

"Yes, this is what I want to say. Although there is love in my life too. I love my children, but the irony is that my children are the product of compulsion and not of any love," saying this Kaiksee took a deep breath. She looked very tired.

"How much pain is there in your heart, Kaikasi," saying this Mani wiped away the tears welling up in Kaikasi's eyes with her lap.

"You are right Mani, there is indeed a lot of pain within me, but there is also a rebellion somewhere, although it has never been vocal. Like pain, rebellion also remained stifled within."

Kaikasi kept her head in Mani's lap and sobbed. Mani placed her hand on Kaikasi's head. After some time, when Kaikasi raised his head, there were lines of tears on her cheeks. Mani cleaned Kaiksi's face with his fingers. After a few moments-

"Mani, perhaps this is the reason why except Vibhishan, the nature of my other children could not be as per my expectations. Kumbhakarna is very lazy, Suparnakha is very stubborn and Ravan is very brave, courageous and intelligent, he is also studying Vedas from his father, but at the same time, he also seems to be foolish. I feel worried about his future too because due to foolishness, even virtues give the same results as vices," Kaikasi said.

(In future, Ravan also commented on the verses of the Vedas, edited them interpreting their mantras. This work of Ravan came to be known as 'Krishna Yajurveda'. Veda recitation was very popular and appreciated in Ravan's Lanka.)

"You said that your children are not the product of love but of compulsion. Have you never been able to love Vishrava?"

"The love you are talking about, Mani, is a combination of compassion, sympathy, and sexual attraction. There was neiher compassion nor sympathy and I could never develope any kind of attraction towards him."

"You must have had some feelings towards him?'

"Emotions require cause and effect. So, the cause was the birth of a son from him, and the effect was my life becoming devoid of interest. Hence I will not be able to say what kind of feelings were there. Mani you can understand me."

"Maybe you don't know it well, but there seems some hatred towards him hidden in some corner of your mind."

"No, for hatred it is necessary to have anger, fear and aversion towards someone. I had and still have a dislike for him in my mind, but there was neither anger nor fear.

"How come but you have become very knowledgeable?"

"No, not knowledgeable one, don't say so, but yes life has taught me a lot".

"I have one more question."

"And what is that?''

"During our conversation for so long, you addressed your husband only by his name 'Vishrava'. No words like 'pati', 'Muni' or 'Rishi' were used for him, why?"

"I have completed the marriage ceremony with him, but for me, that ceremony was always just a process to get a son as per the father's orders, so that he can regain his respect in the society. Marriage is the union of two souls, Mani. Vishrva is just a man to me and I am just a woman to him, that's all."

"Oh!'' Mani said.

"But Mani, if there exists a dark side to anything, there must be a bright siade too. The bright side of this whole incident is that curiosity about life and the tendency for self-reflection has increased in me."

"What sort of philosopher are you becoming?"

"Do not use grandiloquent language with me, Mani, but consider how dull and unappealing a life devoid of emotion must be. I am a mother, yet I am grateful to God for guiding me towards this reflection, thus preventing my life from becoming colourless."

"What colour is it, Kaikasi?"

"I have nothing left to worry about, regarding my family. Vishrava is fully capable of taking care of himself, and the children are being guided by their grandfather and eleven uncles. Beyond all this, there is so much in the earth and sky to observe and comprehend, it has started to feel pleasant."

"Ok then," Mani replied.

Upon reaching adulthood, Ravan, along with Kumbhakarna, Surpanakha, and Vibhishana, departed from Vishrava's hermitage to accompany Sumali. Although their father, Vishrava, was reluctant to send Ravan with Sumali, he had imparted education and values to Ravan in accordance with the sage's traditions. Vishrava was aware of Sumali's devious intentions and had an understanding of Ravan's capabilities. He was concerned about the welfare of society as well as Ravan's future, yet he found himself helpless before Sumali aggressiveness.

By entering into an alliance with Sumali, Ravana completely came under his influence. He accomplished the goal set by his maternal grandfather Sumali, defeated Kubera, took over Lanka and eventually became its sovereign ruler.

3.
Amid Emotions

Ram's flow of thoughts broke, he got up, went to the balcony outside the room and started looking towards the sky. It was sunset time. Some dark clouds were floating. It seemed as if they wanted to cover the sky soon. A sense of tranquility washed over him, and he felt a slight easing of his troubled mind. He then turned his attention to Sita.

'Sita, are you hidden somewhere in this sky?' he said in his mind and this thought made him chuckle softly in himself.

Thinking, 'Life has become so incomplete,' he slightly lowered his eyelids, bit his lips, raised the palm of his left hand a little towards the sky, once again let out a painful laugh, and then opened his eyes.

Clouds had covered almost the entire sky. There was very little light left. The dusk was about to fall. The trees seemed to be full of shadows.

The wind was strong and cold. Suddenly it started raining heavily. The downpour, accompanied by the gusts, soaked him, suddenly a lone bird came flying out and making noise. He laughed again. He was also alone amidst the rain, hail and strong winds. The bird had come and gone. Now there was no voice. Ram felt that Sita had already gone facing such strong and unfavorable winds and now he had to face the same strong winds. Sita had left him. How lonely and hurt he was. He had suffered many traumas in his life, but the blow of Sita's departure was unbearable for him.

Whenever this story of Ayodhya will be written, Sita will be its silent pillar. She had never asked any questions anywhere.

“Seete, are you silence itself?’’ Ram said internally.

He remembered that he and Sita were introduced as husband and wife, but soon he started feeling that the bond between them was not of bodies but of souls. This was the pinnacle of love and trust.

‘Seete, you embody love and faith. Whatever happened during the Ashwamedha Yagya, must have been so painful for you.

This was once again a question mark on your chastity and you, who had endured so many pains throughout your life, could not bear this pain and chose to depart,’ Ram said in his mind.

Right then there was a very strong lightning. Ram looked towards the sky. The clouds had thinned and the blue of the sky was becoming visible. Calling out ‘Sita, where are you?’ in himself Ram closed his eyes and when he opened them after some time, it seemed as if Sita was watching him from the sky, visible in between the shadows of the trees. He was wondered, rubbed his eyes and then confirmed that it was indeed Sita with Shining face and in plain yellow clothes. In the same clothes, she had come to Ashwamedha Yagya from Valmiki’s ashram.

“Seete you there,” he said anxiously.

“Yes, it is me,” she said and smiled.

“Where are you ?’’

“There,’’ Sita raised her finger and pointed towards him. Ram could not understand anything. He looked around and then asked again,

“Where?’’

“There it-self,’’ Sita again pointed towards them.

“I can’t understand, Sita, where are you?’’

"Raghukula Nandan, why don't you put your hand on your chest and look inside yourself?"

"Oh,'' he laughed and saw Sita too was laughing. Ram stood there lost in that laughter for some time, then said,

"Seete, keep laughing like this forever and please don't go.''

"I myself don't want to go,'' she replied.

Right then a piece of cloud came, went to where Sita was visible, covered her completely and flew away. After it left, Ram saw that Sita was not there. It was only a clear sky.

Ram had been standing for a long time. He started looking for a place to sit. He soptted something to sit, on a corner of the balcony.

It was still raining, varying in intensity and due to the strong winds the drops were drenching him persistently.

With a childlike mind, he turned the palm of one hand towards the sky and started feeling the touch of the water drops falling on it. It seemed pleasant.

Sita's laughter was not leaving Ram's mind. This laughter had always tickled his heart. Even today the same thing had happened for a few moments but as soon as Sita left, he had become sad. He vividly recalled the first time he had seen her, her laughter still resonating in his memory, a moment he had never forgotten.

He recalled the time when in Janakpuri, along with Lakshman, he had accidentally entered the garden where Sita used to come daily. On that evening also she had come with her friends and was engrossed in some joke. The joy radiated from her, illuminating her face, her lips resembling the delicate petals of a flower, and her smile revealing a row of gleaming teeth. In Ram's eyes, the world had seemed to come alive.

Upon catching sight of Sita, he was momentarily taken aback, standing there in a daze. His gaze shifted from her enchanting smile just as Sita turned to look at him. Overwhelmed with nervousness, he eventually retreated, yet his thoughts remained tied to the sound of her laughter.

The rain had slowed down, but the droplets continued to fall. Suddenly lightning flashed again and a lot of light scattered like the light that sita's laughter used to bring. Ram's pain deepened. Sita had taken away that light with herself.

Searching for her, Ram's eyes again stopped at the same place in the sky where Sita had been seen some time ago. Behind the group of trees there was only the sky and nothing else, but for some unknown reason, Ram felt that there was some light there. Looking at it, he entered a contemplative state.

The same bird once again passed by making noise and screaming.

Ram tried to see it but it was not visible. He felt as though his own mind echoed a cry for Sita, only to settle into silence.

It was still raining at the same pace. He got up and walked slowly, standing under the open sky and getting wet. He didn't feel like going to the room.

Ram remembered how Sita, hurt by the question raised on her chastity, had quickly and very quietly left the yagya place for some unknown place, saying a lot to him with her eyes.

What was there in those eyes? What might Sita have said? Ram remembered that there were signs of love, reproach, farewell and a lot of emptiness in those eyes.

There was such a big void in the eyes which were always sparkled with laughter. Remembering how distraught he had become at that time, he felt the same again today.

'So what if you can't come to me, I shall come to you," he contemplated silently.

Again your dense shadow
Has faded away
And I am left
In this sizzling sunshine
Standing all alone.

xxxxxxx

Ram had been here for a long time. Lakshman, after searching for Ram in almost all the rooms, came to the roof of the palace. He was astonished to see Ram drenched in rain, standing in the dark under the open sky. After Sita's departure, the detachment that was sometimes visible in Ram's behaviour used to worry him. 'This is natural and with the passage of time the wounds in his heart will heal', this thought provided him some comfort, yet witnessing Ram in this state today left him so bewildered that he could not utter a word, remaining speechless as he gazed at him. Ram's posture remained unchanged despite the relentless thunder and flashing lightning. Lakshman observed him for a while before approaching and gently touching his shoulder, saying, "Brother."

Ram was startled by this sudden touch. Looked at Lakshman and said,

"Oh! Lakshman.''

"Brother, you are very wet, let's go downstairs."

A lot was going on in Lakshman's mind, but he did not find this opportunity appropriate to say it all. Both came down. Lakshman ordered clothes from a maid and gave them to Ram. Ram went to a room and came out after drying his body and changing his clothes. Lakshman himself had got wet. He also changed his clothes. By then a fire had been lit at one place.

Both Ram and Lakshman sat near the fire.

The stillness of the night was deep. No one was saying anything but there was an unspoken tension. After some time Lakshman broke the silence,

"Brother, what has happened to you, standing alone at night at this hour and getting wet in the rain?"

Ram did not give any answer to this, only a faint smile was on his lips. Lakshman continued to watch him for some time and then said,

"Brother, Bhabhi (sister-in-law) is no more."

"Yes thai is it, Lakshman."

"If she were here, would she have allowed you to do this?"

After some time Lakshman again said,

"But brother, she is very much here."

Ram laughed at this and said,

"Yes, Lakshman she is.''

It had been some time since they were sitting,

"Brother, my heart too aches deeply over my Bhabhi's departure." Lakshman said looking at Ram.

Ram chose not to respond, merely averting his gaze. Sensing Ram's unspoken feelings, Lakshman stepped closer, took Ram's hand in his own, and remarked, "This sorrow is not yours alone."

At this, Ram turned his attention to Lakshman and said, "I understand, Lakshman." As he lowered his eyelids, tears formed at their edge. This sight moved Lakshman profoundly, prompting him to draw nearer to Ram.

"Brother, please forgive me. I did not mean to hurt you," he pleaded.

"No, Lakshman, it is nothing of the sort," Ram replied, attempting a smile that fell short.

"The tears of someone whose gallantry can hardly be described in words are not my illusion." Lakshman continued.

"Who is not affected by states of happiness or sorrow? And sometimes shedding tears is perhaps better for a person than swallowing them, but some people are not even allowed to bring tears in their eyes. How tragic it is."

"Some individuals possess such greatness that others expect only guidance from their eyes and not tears," Lakshman added.

"You may express it however you wish," Ram said, trying to laugh.

"It is very late, go and sleep," saying this Ram got up and went towards his bedroom. Lakshman also got up.

Upon entering his own room, Lakshman found Urmila waiting for him. "The weather is turning quite severe," she remarked.

"Yes," he replied.

"You are very late," she noted.

"Brother was feeling very sorrowful," Lakshman explained, sharing his concerns about Ram.

"His grief is understandable, but standing in such a state of distress..." Urmila responded.

xxxxxxx

Ram entered his bedroom and became immersed in memories of Sita for a while before gradually lying down on the bed. Sleep began to envelop his weary mind and body, and soon a dream started to take shape in his vision.

In a vast kingdom, there lived a courageous prince who had learned from his mentors about a fairy princess residing far beyond the dense forest and towering mountains. One day, he took a magnificent and swift horse from his palace to seek out this fairy, mounted the horse and set off on his journey.

As the prince traversed the forest, he heard a faint groan. He halted and scanned his surroundings. When the sound echoed again, he followed it. Approaching closer, he discovered a woman lying on her side, moaning in agony, with a knife embedded in her back. The pain rendered her unable to move.

The prince gathered some herbs from the forest, ground them, with great care, he removed the knife from her back and applied the mixture to her wounds. Then he went and brought some water on a folded leaf and offered it to her to drink.

Once the woman's pain began to ease, the prince lifted her onto his horse and transported her to her home. She had been attacked by robbers, and her husband had shown indifference, blaming her only for the incident. The prince felt a deep sorrow in his heart.

"How can you be so unkind?" the prince said to her husband. After the husband acknowledged his error and promised to care for his wife in the future, the prince continued on his journey. One day, while traversing the forest and mountains, he encountered the fairy.

They exchanged glances, engaged in conversation, sat together, and soon became enamored with one another. As the prince prepared to return, he invited the fairy to accompany him. The fairy agreed, saying, "You may ride your horse; I will come flying."

"You will struggle in vain; the path is fraught with high mountains and dense forests. I cannot allow you to wander alone," the prince replied.

"Then?" she said.

"My horse is strong and swift. Please ride with me, and we shall travel together."

The fairy sat on the horse. While they were crossing the mountain, a very strong black storm came. It was pitch dark. They stood behind a rock. The fairy had never seen such a terrible storm. She was very scared. Her fear increased even more when after the storm stopped, a man with an axe on his shoulder and full of anger came and stood in front of them. The fairy, frightened, stood behind the prince. That man started staring at the prince with his bloodshot eyes as if he would burn him in the fire of his anger. The fairy was unable to understand why that man was doing this. She looked towards the prince. He was standing motionless and fearless, looking at that man and perhaps was smiling a little.

The man glared at the prince with bloodshot eyes, as if he intended to unleash his fury upon him. The fairy was perplexed by the man's hostility and looked to the prince for reassurance. He stood resolute and unafraid, gazing at the man, perhaps even offering a slight smile.

This smile seemed to temper the man's rage. He uttered an "Oh," as if he had come to a realization, then turned and vanished back into the trees and mountains. No harm came to them, and the prince resumed his journey to the city with the fairy.

They spent a long time living in the city. Most people loved and respected them a lot, but some people were jealous of them and one day when the prince was not there, those people threw stones at the fairy and hurt her a lot. The fairy fell down badly injured and started moaning. After this, the people who threw stones at her, ran away fearing the arrival of the prince.

The prince came. He was filled with sorrow and anger on seeing the fairy. The injured fairy was not ready to stay there any longer. Despite the prince's attempts to stop her, she flew away and disappeared into the sky.

After the fairy left, the prince became very sad. He sat on the horse and went out of the city, left the horse, crown, precious clothes, ornaments etc. and started walking towards the forest barefoot. A river came on the way. The prince climbed the bridge built on it to cross it. He was almost midway when the bridge broke and the prince fell into the river.

The dream broke and Ram was shocked. 'Is this a sign of the future?' a thought came to his mind. At first, he smiled a little, opened his lips, and then, not knowing why, he started laughing.

4.
Public Opinion

A considerable amount of time had passed since Sita's departure. The citizens of Ayodhya, who had played a role in her condemnation, were now filled with regret and had lost their respect not only in society but also in the eyes of their own families.

There were two kinds of stories prevalent regarding Sita's departure. There were many who said that she was the daughter of the earth and Mother Earth had sent a golden throne on which she sat and disappeared into the earth. However, there were also many who said that she had disappeared into the sky by becoming invisible.

The empire of Ayodhya had expanded to a great extent and Ram's influence had also spread far and wide, but Sita had not only become a topic of discussion but also an object of people's reverence Many people had Sita's idols in their homes, where she had taken the place of a goddess and was the center of faith in the minds of people.

A residence in Ayodhya was owned by Manas and Chitra, both of whom were ardent devotees of Sita. On that particular day, Manas was engaged in worship. In front of him were statues of Shiva and Parvati, accompanied by a picture of Sita. Chitra had her eyes closed, her face radiating a gentle glow, complemented by a faint smile. After a while, when Chitra opened her eyes, Manas regarded her with a curious expression.

"Mother was present," Chitra remarked with a laugh.

"Mother?" he inquired.

"Yes, she was Sita."

"Oh."

"Very well, now please rise and let me take your place," Manas responded.

"But I wish to remain seated a little longer," Chitra replied and closed her eyes once again, straightened her posture, and immersed herself in prayer. After some time, she uttered, "Mother, your emotions and blessings are beyond words." Thus paying her respects to Sita she stood up. She had some household chores to attend.

5.
And She Came But......

Ram came out of the palace with reluctance and took his seat in the chariot, instructing the charioteer to take him to the location where Sita's footprints had last been found. The chariot began its journey. Ram was sitting in silence, deep in thoughts. Soon, they arrived at the site.

There was a grove of trees, and beneath one of them lay the sacred footprints of Sita. The area was revered, with worshippers tying red threads around the tree and leaving flowers at its base. It was a peaceful and attractive place, full with a sense of holiness. Ram often used to come to this spot and sit for some time. Today, upon his arrival, he noticed an abundance of blooming flowers. He sat quietly, gazing at the flowers for a while before closing his eyes.

He remained sitting in silence for a considerable period, then in his thoughts he called out, "Sita," which brought a faint smile to his lips, as if he were anticipating her arrival. After a while, he repeated, 'Sita, please come.' Yet, there was no response; Sita did not appear. Moments later, Ram smiled again and asked, "Sita, are you angry?" And he felt as if Sita is there before him. He started looking at her.

After a brief pause, Sita remarked,

"Will you just sit silently and keep looking at me or will you say something?"

"Yes I will. A lot is there to say."

"Then please come out."

"But I don't know, from where to start."

"Start from anywhere."

"Sita, when I had seen you for the first time in the garden of Janakpuri then…."

"Then what?" Sita said.

"After you looked at me, surprised I looked away and the thirst to see you remained in my heart."

"Oh," Sita laughed.

"Yes and even after living with you for such a long time, my feelings are the same."

"Even now?"

"Yes, even now and one more thing," Ram said.

"And what is that?"

"I have seen you, I have lived with you, but …."

"But what?"

"Many people have a big heart, but but you are an exception."

"Is that so," she smiled.

"Your heart is so big that one life is not enough to see it."

Now Sita laughed out heartly. She said,

"Very often, the things depend on the mind of viewer."

"You have accepted all the sorrows and happiness of life with such an ease. You never complained about anything, this is the true greatness," Ram said.

"Raghukulanandan, I feel you are flowing in the sea of emotions."

"Although this is not mere sentimentality, it is true, still Sita, let this Ram too, get emotional atleast occasionally."

"Why are you saying this? I have always found you very emotional."

"How is it Sita? I was always bound by my royal duties and responsibilities. I never gave any importance to my personal feelings."

"Are you sad?"

"No, but sometimes when I see you, I feel like getting carried away by emotions."

Sita laughed and said,

"What a good fortune I have," Sita said before looking at him with some surprise.

Throught her life, Sita had primarily perceived Ram as serious and bound by responsibilities. Today his face was serious, but it also looked as simple as a small child's. It appeared as if an innocent child was speaking his mind. Silence prevailed for a while, only the sound of the wind passing through the trees could be heard. Then Ram said,

"Sita."

"Yes."

"After returning from Ravan's captivity, when your character was questioned for the first time, if I had shown even a little harshness at that time, listening to the voice of my heart, then no one would could to discuss it for a second time."

Sita also became serious on this note. In a moment, many memories flashed before her eyes.

"Perhaps," Sita replied.

"Not perhaps Sita, but for sure. No one on the earth has the courage to face my anger."

"Yes indeed."

"Then Valmiki Ashram would not have come in your life. Luv and Kush would not have to spend their childhood without a father and........."

"And?"

"Whatever had happened in the Ashvamedha Yagna would not have happened and I would not have been so alone."

"You are not alone, I am with you wherever I am, and you do not need to regret anything. It was very clear how much you were distressed by whatever was happening at the Yagna-sthal and when I was leaving that place, I had seen deep pain in your eyes. Those were very distressing moments indeed."

Ram was still very emotional. He said,

"How much pain must have been in your mind at that time."

"No, there was no pain."

"No pain? But how can you say so," Ram said.

"Because there was no desire or reluctance left in my mind," Sita said.

Ram became silent after this answer. Sita said again,

"Sometimes the mind becomes so detached and emotionless that it becomes completely calm and reaction less."

"Yes, sometimes the injury is so intense and deep that the feeling of pain vanishes for some time."

"Injury! But I was not injured in any way." Sita said smilingly to reduce the seriousness of the atmosphere.

"I am not talking about the injury to the body, Sita."

"Still, why are you so worried?"

"Sita, will you sit with me for some time more?"

"Yes, I will sit and say something," Sita said.

"Yes, please speak out."

Sita sat down beside Ram and facing him.

"Shall I begin?" he said.

"Yes please."

"Sadness and happiness are states of mind, shouldn't we come out of these?"

"You are right Sita and I am seeing that I am getting more and more under the control of emotions."

"And this feeling of 'I am the doer'? This leads you to say that I did this or did not accomplish that."

"True."

"And why this anger? Why not that innocent peace that is within us?"

"Sita, I feel that getting angry at injustice is virtuous anger. If we do not get angry even at injustice, then the morale of the unjust will embolden."

"You are right. Anger at injustice is natural and appropriate, but is it necessary?"

"Mitigation of injustice is necessary, isn't it? Anger gives it direction.''

"But there is always a high possibility that anger will give it the wrong direction. But whatever you did was quite appropriate according to the time. Then why this voice of regret?''

Ram did not reply on it. He just looked at Sita like a disciple looks at his Guru. When their eyes met, Sita said again,

"Come out of this state of mind. We can neither be destroyed nor can we die. We are either nothing or everything. Me and God, are there two,?''

Sita said. Ram was listening quietly. Sita finished saying

"Why are you so silent?''

"You are correct,'' Ram said. Then he paused for a while and then added, "True, I was distracted for some time.''

"Come out of the sorrow of my departure. I have not gone."

Ram looked at Sita and she said,

"Truly speaking, I am with you all the time," then she laughed and said,

"You have said many times that you are afraid of my anger."

"Yes, I am," saying this Ram smiled.

"If you do not laugh and keep sitting serious like this, I will become angry."

"No, please don't," Ram laughed in response.

"Well, then may I leave now," said Sita.

Just then a bird passed by flapping its wings and making noise as if someone had scared it and made it fly away. Ram's eyes opened. There was nothing except the trees and some flowers lying on the ground.

"Oh," saying this he stood up as if he had just woken up from sleep, but his mind was very light and peaceful.

Someone appeared
In dreams
Awake and laughing
And asking too
To wake up.

6.
This Side Too

Luv and Kush had grown up. Whenever their mother was discussed, expressions of pain would easily appear on their faces. The place where Sita had disappeared had become like a temple for them. They would often come here. Today when they came, Ram was also there.

"Come," Ram said upon noticing them.

Luv and Kush greeted him respectfully, having brought flowers along. They placed the flowers at the Seete dedicated to their mother and after mentally offering their respects, they bowed and touched that ground with their forehead.

"Are you coming from the palace?" Ram inquired.

"Yes," they both replied almost in unison.

"Let us sit here for a while," Ram suggested, taking Luv's hand, the younger one of the two in his hand. Nearby, there was a slightly elevated spot where all the three took a seat.

Surrounded by lush greenery, the atmosphere was serene as the sun had begun to set. A gentle coolness and the fragrance of the greenry had filled the air. Some squirrels were climbing trees nearby. Ram started watching them. Just then a squirrel came jumping, paused near Ram's feet, touched them and ran away.

"Oh, you," Ram exclaimed.

"Who is it?" Kush asked. When Luv and Kush were together, Luv often remained silent, perhaps as a sign of respect for his elder brother.

"Nothing, just a squirrel," Ram replied.

"But the way you said 'Oh, you' made it sound as if you were greeting a friend," Kush said.

"These squirrels seem quite familiar to me,"said Ram laughingly. Luv and Kush seemed a little surprised by this answer.

"How is it so, Father?" Kush inquired.

"During our time in exile, we encountered squirrels everywhere. They would bounce and leap about, which greatly entertained your mother. She often fed them, and we would sometimes sit beneath a tree, watching their playful antics."

Luv and Kush smiled at this.

"Is that so?" Luv asked.

"Yes, indeed. And Kush, when we were building a bridge over the sea to free your mother from Ravan's captivity, a squirrel was bringing pebbles in its mouth as if it was helping in that work."

"Oh," Kush and lav responded with a smile.

"At times, these squirrels evoke memories of the past," Ram continued.

The atmosphere had become somewhat serious after the topic of Sita being held in Lanka came up. Ram sensed this, addressed Luv and Kush and said,

"You both seem to have grown a bit serious, Kush."

"And you too Father," Kush replied.

"Seriousness is my nature, Kush."

"Mother used to say that you were always somewhat serious, but not excessively so," Luv added.

Ram smiled at this observation.

"What else did she say?"

"She used to tell us a lot about you. Especially that you were not only an ideal character, but also took great care of her."

"Is that so?"

"Indeed, Father. Whenever she discussed you, it was as if she were in another world. She shared numerous insights about your character and deeds."

"Kush, surely she must have had some grievances as well."

"No, her heart was filled with admiration for you."

"Very well," Ram replied and with a faint smile gracing his lips as he added,

"Still, she must have complained about something at some point.

"Yes she had a complaint against you."

"Is that so?" Ram inquired. "Please, share with me the grievance she had against me."

"She used to say that you neglect your own well-being."

`"Indeed, that is a big complaint," Ram laughed heartly.

"But she was always there to look after me," he added.

"Yes, this is what he was worried about while staying in Maharishi Valmiki's ashram. She always wondered who would have been taking care of you now."

On hearing Sita's concern for him even in Valmiki's ashram, Ram softly said 'hmm' and then he became serious again.

A moment of silence ensued, until Luv, who had remained mostly quiet throughout the discussion, spoke up,

"Father."

"Yes?"

"A question frequently arises in our minds."

"What is it?"

"Why did Mother and you make such a difficult decision based solely on the saying of one individual?"

"He was not merely one person; there were several individuals involved. But yes, only one person had uttered such words."

"Yet they were still just a few."

"Indeed, my dear, they were a few, but there was also a growing sentiment regarding us."

"That may be true, but there could have been alternative ways to reddress that sentiment, Dad," Kush remarked.

"Kush, do you believe that they could have been appeased through conversation?"

"Yes, I think so."

"Some individuals had attempted this."

"Then?

"When individuals with malicious intent protest merely for the sake of protesting, they will remain unyielding despite numerous facts and attempts to persuade them."

"Was he harboring malicious intent?

"Only someone with ill will could question the integrity of a woman like your mother, Kush."

Kush became silent, and inhaled deeply, as he felt a profound pain within.

"Kush there were alternative methods to dismiss those words as trivial and that individual could have been silenced through some punishment. At worst he could be awarded a death penalty and a message could have been conveyed to those who spoke out such things."

"Indeed, various actions could have been taken," Kush acknowledged.

"But however, such actions do not extinguish the underlying idea; rather, they may cause it to generate in different forms, potentially worsening the situation."

"It is conceivable that this could have occurred, necessitating further measures, but a pregnant woman would not have been forced to take the decision of leaving the home. Was that the only option left?" Kush said.

"Yes, I understand that this question must be arising in the minds of many others too and it is likely continue in the future, allowing some individuals to cast blame upon me."

Neither Kush nor Luv responded to it.

"However, there is one more aspect, Kush," Ram said.

"And what is it?

"In the pursuit of fulfilling societal responsibilities, individuals often find themselves compelled to prioritize the needs of the community over their own personal interests and those of their familiy. This phenomenon has occurred in the past and will undoubtedly continue in the future too." And this statement led Ram to fall into a contemplative silence.

Kush and Lav remained silent. They did not respond. Ram felt as if they had found this point correct, but there was still some resistance and considerable emotional turmoil.

"It is good that you raised this question in front of me today. I myself also wanted to talk to you about this.

Kush, we both were very hurt by the discussion about her character once again. The pain it caused us was so profound that we could not sleep that night. We spent the entire night walking. I will never forget that night."

Probebly the recollection of these matters was causing Ram considerable distress, and so his voice became somewhat heavy.

"Our hearts were filled with extreme disgust towards the power and the crooked politics of the palaces. It was this politics, due to whose curse my father died an untimely death, I, along with your mother and Lakshman spent fourteen years in the dense forests of Dandakaranya in the far south and your mother had to spend thirteen months in Ravan's captivity.

Every person in our family has suffered a lot from this sting of crooked politics."

Having said this, Ram paused for a few moments and then he continued,

"Your mother expressed a desire to leave the palaces. And when she mentioned this intention to depart, I resolved to accompany her. However, she was not ready for this decision of mine, as none of Bharat, Lakshman, or Shatrughan was equipped to manage the kingdom under those circumstances. Ayodhya could not be abandoned to its fate, as that could constitute a renunciation of our duties and could prove fatal."

Luv and Kush listened attentively, recalling their time at Valmiki Ashram, where their mother imparted lessons on the virtues and responsibilities of kingship. They were made to understand that despite their upbringing in the sage's ashram, they would eventually be called upon to wield royal authority.

They remembered their mother's teachings, emphasizing that a king must not hesitate to sacrifice personal and familial interests for the greater good of the people and adherence to royal duties. Previously, they had struggled to grasp the significance of her words, but following this conversation with their father, they not only began to comprehend their meaning but also recognized the pain and sacrifices his father had endured.

Tears welled in their eyes as Ram made these revelations. Observing this Ram tried to console them.

"The decision of your mother to go to Maharishi Valmiki's ashram was the result of this pain of ours; however, it is important to recognize that, despite the absence of a palace and similar amenities, the ashram was far from ordinary. Situated on the banks of the Ganga, it was a sacred place associated with a revered saint like Maharishi Valmiki. The environment was filled with pleasant, knowledgeable, well-mannered, and compassionate individuals. There your mother could live free from many tensions, which was very necessary for a pregnant woman. Moreover you people got the company of Maharishi Valmiki since your childhood. This early association with Maharishi Valmiki contributed significantly to your character development and is indeed a matter of great significance.

Ram's words served as a soothing balm for the wounds of Luv and Kush.

"Indeed, you are correct," they acknowledged.

"Are there any further questions?" Ram inquired.

"No, Father, there are no more questions," Kush replied.

"However, since our discussion has concluded, I would like to share something else also," Ram stated.

"And what is that?"

"This pertains to Dandakaranya, the place where we lived during our exile and from where your mother was abducted."

"Yes, Father, please tell me about that," Luv asked eagerly.

"That place was once ruled by a foolish and uneducated king Danda. Once that king found Aarja, the daughter of demons' Guru Shukracharya, alone and forcefully behaved immorally with her. This infuriated Shukracharya and the demons completely destroyed his empire and established their supremacy over it and turned it into a jungle. Later, Ravana took it under his supremacy and gave it to his sister Surpanakha. This jungle was called Dandakaranya after the name of King Danda.''

"It was very nice to know this from you," said Kush.

"There is one more thing, Kush," Ram added.

"What is that?"

Some individuals claim that I had killed Shambuk because he was a Shudra implying that I make distinctions among people based on their varna (cast).

"Indeed, we have heard this," came the response.

"But however they don't consider one thing. If I could take the life of the innocent Shambuk while he was engaged in penance on the basis of caste, then I could also eliminate the individual, who was washerman by cast and who had made such a grave accusation against Sita, which hit to our lives miserably. Why did I not get him killed?

And Kusha, also think about why I gave my consent to your mother going to the ashram of the avarna Maharshi Valmiki instead of sending her to the ashram of a Brahmin sage like Agastya who is said to have conquered the ocean. There were other Brahmin sages too? Were the doors of those other ashrams closed for us or could there have been any threat to your mother's safety in my presence here?'

"No," Kush replied.

"One thing has to be understood Kush," Ram said and both Kush and Luv looked at him with questioning eyes.

"In this world every person has his own standard to know the truth according to his understanding and his perspective and draws conclusions accordingly.

And this is also a bitter truth that lies are more nimble and spread faster than truth, but no matter how much truth is twisted and attacked, it keeps burning and shining like a fire particle somewhere and sometimes when the things are exposed, the truth can be very different and shocking from the beliefs." Ram said.

"That is indeed true," Kush and Luv concurred.

The atmosphere had become serious and gloomy due to the talk of Sita's sufferings. It was evening. They got up and headed towards the chariots to return to the palace.

xxxxxxx

Numerous events, such as the slaying of Tadka, the breaking of Shiva's bow during Sita's Swayamvar, and the escape of Parshuram, contributed to the public perception of Ram as a formidable prince.

On the other hand, the normalisation of Ahalya who was turned into stone, his behaviour with the boatman to ferry him across the river, eating the leftover berries of an ordinary tribal woman but not hurting her feelings, etc. were the incidents due to which he had started ruling over the hearts of the people.

The defeat of Ravan and Kumbhakarna, along with the expansion of Ayodhya's influence in southern India, further solidified his status as a powerful and respected emperor. Throughout this extensive journey, Ram encountered numerous challenges, endured hardships, and got engaged in battles. Despite never experiencing defeat, the departure of Sita had left him feeling as though he had lost everything.

Ram, who had never lost patience in life, felt as if his patience was waning. He felt an overwhelming urge to weep for his perceived loss, yet societal constraints prevented him from expressing his sorrow openly, leaving his anguish trapped within. After this discussion with Luv and Kush, when Ram returned to the palace, he was engulfed by memories of Sita. He entered his chamber and stood by the window, gazing at the vast sky before him, closing his eyes as if to capture its essence within himself.

We had met after a long gap
There was a lot
To hear and say
But why does it happen
That our hearts are lost
Listening
To the footsteps of time
And things slip away
From our hands

He remembered that after Sita had taken refuge Valmiki Ashram, and when he thought that Sita would be living in a hut there, he had decided that he would also live in a hut while performing all the royal duties and then he got a hut built in the rear part of the palace and started living in it. There were only a few simple household items and a mat was his bed for those twelve long years.

Although Sita going to Valmiki Ashram and Ram staying in Ayodhya to fulfill his duties, happened with the consent of both of them, still somewhere in Ram's mind there was a deep pain about Sita leaving the house like this and then not being able to support her in that condition.

Living in a hut by reducing all his needs used to reduce his pain and now after Sita leaving the world, Ram's mind was filled with a feeling of detachment towards the world. Although responsibilities were not allowing him to leave everything and take up renunciation, yet this feeling was repeatedly coming out in his words and behaviour.

Sometimes he used to feel that his mind has become like a piece of cloud flying in the sky, which has no desire to go in any direction. Only the sense of duty had remained behind all his actions.

In his life after marriage, he had been separated from Sita twice. Once, when she was in Ravan's captivity and the second time, when Sita was in Valmiki's Ashram for twelve years.

He remembered that during the time Sita was away from him, he used to think about what she would have said if she was here. How would she have felt? Ram always hoped and waited to meet Sita. Any thought of meeting her used to make Ram restless, but now, when Sita had left this world, those feelings were lost somewhere alongwith all the attachments.

Ram was overwhelmed by the determination that Sita had shown even at that young age in Ravan's captivity and then the selfless way in which she had spent twelve years in Valmiki's ashram.

When the thought of Ravan came to his mind, he also remembered that Ravan himself was the son of a woman who was a victim of the injustice of men, but still he himself never hesitated in doing injustice to women.

7.
Sunshine And Shadows Too

On that particular day, upon returning home in the evening after a long and exhausting day at work, Ram entered his room to find the servants waiting as usual, ready with fresh clothes for him to change into and water for washing his hands and feet.

After cleansing himself and changing attire, he felt a sense of rejuvenation. Just as he settled into his seat, refreshments were brought to him. He reached out to take some, but a touching thought struck him: had Sita been there, she would have been by his side at this moment.

In the past, Sita was not only present during his returns but also took great intrest in preparation of refreshments for him. This memory flooded back to him, and he was suddenly reminded of his return from Lanka. Vividly, the scene unfolded in his mind, depicting the journey he and Sita had undertaken from Lanka to Ayodhya after completion of their exile.

There were countless stories and questions they both wished to share, but in the Pushpak Viman, they were surrounded by Lakshman, Hanuman, and Vibhishan, so they maintained a serious posture, unable to express their thoughts to one another.

Ram recalled that as soon as he found a moment of solitude, he approached Sita, taking her hand in his and asking, “Seete.”

She replied, “yes.”

He then inquired, “How did so many days pass?”

In response to this, Sita looked at Ram. Their eyes locked, and Sita then embraced Ram tightly, weeping uncontrollably. Ram, unable to restrain himself, found tears filling his eyes despite his efforts to remain composed.

Upon witnessing Ram's tears, Sita momentarily forgot her own sorrow. Both of them used her garment to dry their tears, exchanged glances, and then unexpectedly burst into laughter.

"But why are we weeping now?" Ram inquired.

"Yes indeed," Sita replied, and they both shared a round of laughter.

In the days that followed, whenever they found a moment, they would engage in conversations about their experiences during their exile, particularly focusing on Sita's time in Lanka. One day, during one of these discussions, Ram remarked,

"Sita."

"Yes."

"Sometimes a question crosses my mind."

"And what is it?"

"How did Mandodari come to accept Vibhishana as her husband after Ravan's demise?"

"I believe this question must be in the minds of many," Sita responded.

"Perhaps. Do you have any insight into this matter?"

"I cannot say for certain, but given the circumstances Mandodari faced with Ravan, it does not seem entirely impracticable."

"Under what circumstances?" Ram inquired.

"Let me share whatever I know," Sita replied.

xxxxxxx

A small island situated in the ocean to the south of India was bustling with activity. This island served as the capital of the demon king Makaraksha, who ruled over the surrounding islands. Among his captives were Ravan and a demon girl, the latter of whom harbored deep, albeit unreciprocated, affection for Ravan.

Ravan had sought to establish the Raksha culture, aiming to unify the demons under this new societal framework. In pursuit of this goal, he had engaged himself in a fierce battle against Makaraksha, ultimately resulting in his defeat and subsequent capture. The demon girl was also among those taken prisoner.

When they were being transported by Makaraksha's army across the sea to the capital island, a violent storm erupted, causing numerous boats to capsize. Boats carrying the demon girl, her mother and Ravan were also among the unfortunate vessels. Due to a storm surge Ravan became almost unconscious.

Despite the chaos of the storm, the girl had maintained her composure and, demonstrating remarkable bravery, managed to navigate her boat close to Ravan's. She provided him with support and brought him aboard her vessel. Although Ravan was saved, his mother was tragically consumed by the raging waves.

The intensity of the demon girl's attraction for Ravan was such that she chose to save him over her own mother. This act of sacrifice reached Makaraksha, who then resolved to execute both Ravan and the demon girl when they reached before him.

Following Makaraksha's orders, a demon wielding an axe approached to carry out their execution. His intention was to behead Ravan first, but the demon girl interjected, saying,

"Wait."

The executioner halted, and all eyes in the crowd turned toward her.

"I am a virgin," she declared, "to fulfill your desires, you must sacrifice me first; this way your wishes will soon be realized."

Silence enveloped the scene in response to the girl's plea. Mandodari was also there. Two hearts, those of Ravan and Mandodari, were filled with a profound sense of reverence and sorrow for the unnamed demon girl. The demon wielding the axe glanced at Makaraksh, and upon receiving his nod of approval, approached the demon girl. With a swift swing of the axe, her head was severed, and fell to the ground, blood gushing forth. Ravan shut his eyes in despair, while Mandodari nearly lost consciousness.

Suddenly, a powerful arrow shot by demons of Ravan's side striked that killer demon with remarkable speed and the group of demons that had come to assist Ravan across the sea launched a fierce counterattack against their adversaries. The Seete of the sacrifice transformed into a battlefield.

These unexpectedly arrived demons, initiated a rapid and intense conflict. By the time Makaraksh and his forces could regroup from this surprise assault, numerous demon warriors had already reached Ravan, battling fiercely to clear a path for him.

In a swift turn of events, the demons liberated Ravan. A brutal confrontation ensued, culminating in the death of Makaraksha at the hands of Ravan. The island under Makaraksha's command fell under the dominion of Ravan's Raksha culture.

Next day as dawn broke, Ravan found himself seated near the seashore, his mind racing with thoughts. He was to take control of Makaraksha's entire empire, marking a significant victory for him.

Visions of the sacrifice replayed in Ravan's mind, with the image of the unnamed demon girl haunting him. Her act with selflessness was extraordinary. She had saved Ravan's life on two occasions—once during a tempest at sea and again through her own sacrifice on the island.

In all his life, no one had done such a great sacrifice to Ravan. She loved Ravan, but so many such girls had come in Ravan's life till date. Ravan was overwhelmed by the sacrifice of that demon girl. Her face was repeatedly appearing before Ravan's eyes, requesting the demon to sacrifice her first.

Had she not offered to sacrifice herself before Ravan, Ravan would have become history. God must have sent that girl who saved my life on two occasions. 'I will never forget her,' Ravan contemplated. After wounding Makaraksha, he had thron him alive into the flames.

Even such a terrible revenge was not able to calm his mind and even after such a great victory Ravan was not very happy. The restless Ravan stood up, inhaled deeply, and began to walk, glancing around.

Soon, he noticed an elderly demon approaching him, accompanied by a young girl. Ravan awaited their arrival. In a short time, they drew near.

"Are you Ravan, the son of Vishrava Muni?" inquired the old man.

"Yes," replied Ravan.

"I am May, and this is my daughter Mandodari."

"Are you a demon?" Ravan asked.

"Indeed, but following your victory, I am now your subject," he responded.

"I acknowledge that," said Ravan.

"I have to make a request," the old man continued.

"Please speak out," Ravan urged.

"I am alone and aged; my wife, who was a nymph has departed long ago."

Ravan listened in silence, offering no reply.

"This girl is her daughter."

"Well, Ok"

"I have grown old and wish to be relieved of my responsibilities."

"Tell me how I may assist you," Ravan offered.

"My daughter is exceptionally beautiful and now of marriageable age. I wish for you to accept her as your wife," May stated.

Ravan turned his eyes toward Mandodari, who stood with her head bowed. He was taken aback by that beauty; this daughter of a nymph was indeed as enchanting as a nymph herself.

"I accept your request," he said.

May promptly gathered wood, ignited fire, tied Mandodari's garment to Ravan's attire, securing a knot as he began to chant mantras. Mandodari and Ravan circled the fire seven times, completing the marriage ceremony. May then presented his most formidable weapon to Ravan before taking leave of him.

xxxxxxx

Following Makaraksha's departure, Ravan and Mandodari found themselves alone. The rapid shift in circumstances had left Ravan astonished once more. Just a day prior, he had faced the imminent threat of death.

He felt as though he had returned from a tiring and long journey, utterly fatigued. "Life presents numerous challenges," he mused, settling down quietly like a tired traveler.

Mandodari sat nearby, her head lowered, absentmindedly tracing patterns in the ground with her toe. She awaited some sign of initiative from Ravan, but as the silence lingered, she eventually lifted her gaze to him.

Having witnessed the events at the sacrificial Seete the previous day, Mandodari recalled the fierce determination on Ravan's face even while bound to the altar. In that moment, rather than feeling pity, she found herself admiring him.

Raavan's face was radiant and serious, his arms were strong, his chest was firm and high. He was the possessor of masculine beauty.

"Are you thinking of something?" Mandodari said, pointing at him.

Ravan appeared slightly taken aback.

"Um, yes... no... nothing," he replied.

"Probebly about the war with Makaraksha?" Mandodari said.

"But it has already passed. Were you there yesterday?"

"Yes, and I was very scared too."

"Women have a soft heart, that is probably why this happened."

"But that demon girl was so fearless."

"Yes, she had saved my life twice. If she had not requested the demons to sacrifice her before me, she would have been alive by the time the demons reached there and I would have been dead."

"There must have been a profound affection between the two of you," Mandodari said. However, a hint of feminine jealousy was evident in Mandodari's tone.

Ravan recognized this sentiment and chose not to respond. Mandodari, too, perceived Ravan's silence regarding the matter. After a brief pause, Ravan declared, "I will always remain devoted to her."

"So shall I," Mandodari replied.

At that moment, Ravan turned his gaze toward Mandodari, and he was captivated by her beauty, feeling as though he had never encountered such allure before.

"You surpass any poet's imagination, Mandodari," he remarked, causing her to blush with embarrassment.

"And imagination knows no bounds," Ravan added.

Mandodari lifted her gaze to meet Ravan's. Her expressive eyes conveyed a depth of emotions. Understanding their unspoken language, Ravan took her hand and said,

"And love has no limits Mandodari."

Upon hearing these words, Mandodari slightly raised her head and closed her eyes, pondering, 'Is it truly my fortune to experience love without limits?' The sentiment resonated deeply within her, yet she remained silent.

"You are not responding to my words," Ravan said. Mandodari contemplated, 'What is this feeling?' It was as if she were enveloped in a dream from which she wished never to awaken.

"Please respond, Mandodari," Ravan urged.

"I don't know what to say?" she said.

"I have expressed my feelings, Mandodari," he replied.

"What do you mean by that?" she asked again.

Ravan, uncertain of how to articulate his thoughts, responded, "What do you think?"

"If these are your sentiments only, then why am I feeling their presence and touch?"

"Are you composing poetry?"

"No, but I am absorbing the essence of poetry."

"Then please, say something more."

"I have already conveyed my thoughts."

"When did you do that?"

"Just now."

"But I did not hear anything."

"But I have already spoken," Mandodari insisted.

"Definitely something lacks in my understanding," Ravan said with a laugh, prompting Mandodari to smile gently while covering her lips with her clothe, but unable to conceal the joy in her eyes.

"Your sparkling eyes and smiling lips resonate in my mind like a beautiful melody, Mandodari."

At this remark, shied Mandodari cast her gaze downward in embarrassment. A moment of silence ensued, yet the subtle movement of lips persisted.

There was silence
But the movement of lips
A slight tilt there
And a slant smile
Though for a moment only
Had said a lot

After a brief pause, Ravan spoke again.

"Come, let us depart." They both rose to their feet, with Mandodari trailing behind Ravan. Ravan halted and said,

"Do not follow me but walk alongside me." Mandodari hesitated before responding,

"I have to ask something," she said.

"Yes please, what is that?" he asked.

"It concerns your love for me..." Mandodari left her sentence unfinished.

Ravan grasped her unspoken feelings, affirming,

"You have the sole right", he said

"Truly?"

"Yes, truly and this will always be your prerogative."

Mandodri felt that after this statement of Ravan she had a lot to feel, but nothing to say. She started following Ravan silently.

After walking some distance, Ravana again said,

"Come with me Mandodari, not behind me",

"To follow you is my chosen path."

"No, we must walk together, side by side," Ravan insisted, taking her hand and positioning her beside him. Mandodari felt proud of her good fortune.

xxxxxxx

After a period of time, Ravan launched an assault on Lanka, which was the realm of Kuber. Kuber chose not to confront him and instead sought counsel from his father, Vishrava Muni. Vishrava Muni advised Kuber against engaging in conflict with his brother and recommended that he should abandon Lanka Puri and settle in Alkapuri, located on the Gandhamadan mountains, Kuber followed the advice, allowing Ravan to easily seize control of Lanka.

Ravan had vowed to reserve his affections solely for Mandodari; however as his area of influance expanded, he began to fill his palace with numerous beautiful women. Initially, Mandodari experienced deep sorrow over this development, but over the time she learned to endure it. Still, another event soon brought her great sadness.

8.
Maytanyas

Situated to the south of Dandakaranya, Vyjayantapur was ruled by Asurapati Shambar, a kingdom known for its prosperity. Shambar's wife, Maytanya, daughter of May was a strikingly beautiful young woman, approximately twenty-eight years of age, whose appearance captivated all who beheld her. Her husband, Shambar, was nearly twice her age and primarily occupied with state duties and the intermittent wars that arose.

At present, he was engaged in a conflict between the gods and demons. In this conflict, King Divodas of Panchal and King Dasharatha of Ayodhya allied together, while Shambar and thirty-six Asur kings were infront of them. Accompanying Dasharatha was his wife Kaikeyi, a formidable warrior adept in the art of combat, who was driving Dasharatha's chariot.

Maytanaya was feeling very lonely due to Shambar's absence. She was devoted to Shambar despite the age difference. Maytanaya was sitting sad and lost in thoughts in the courtyard of the palace..

Shambar used to meet Mayatanya and take her leave every time he went to war, but this time he had left without meeting her, and this was no less than a shock for her.

Lost in her thoughts, Maytanaya rose and began to stroll through the garden adjacent to the palace courtyard. With each step taken slowly, her gaze remained fixed on the ground. After a while, she settled down against a tree, resting her head against its trunk while her eyes turned skyward.

After some time, Maytanaya closed her eyes, her mind drifting into memories. She was the elder sister of Mandodari, the wife of Ravan. One day, Ravan unexpectedly arrived in Vaijayantpur. Known for his striking personality, Ravan was considerably younger than Shambar. Shambar received him with great warmth.

Although Ravan was housed in the guest quarters, the bond between Shambar, Maytanaya, and Ravan allowed him the freedom to roam in the palace. Seizing this opportunity, one day Ravan ventured to the entrance of the inner chamber of palace in Shambar's absence. The lady guard stationed at the door attempted to stop him, but Ravan disregarded her, declaring, "I am Ravan."

The guard woman knew about Ravan's relationship with Shambar, so she could not decide immediately and by then Ravan had reached near Mayatnaya. She was taken aback upon seeing Ravan there. She quickly rose to her feet, adjusting her attire, and inquired, "What brings you here, Rakshapati? Is everything all right?"

"I wished to see you," he replied.

"If you had sent word, I would have summoned you," she responded. A sly smile crept across Ravan's face as he remarked,

"Then how could I have witnessed such genuine beauty in its unadulterated form?"

With this statement of Ravan, Maytanaya's face turned red with shame and anger. She said in a sharp voice, "Ravan." Maytanaya's address had both anger and warning.

This voice of hers made Ravan's laughter disappear. He became serious.

"Devi, this was just a joke, but you are beauty personified."

Maytanaya did not give any answer. After some time, when her mind calmed down, she pointed towards a seat and said to Ravan,

"Have a seat."

Ravan sat down. He saw that the expressions of anger on Mayatanya's face were diminishing, so he said again,

"I am infatuated with your beauty, please favour me with…...," and he did not complete the sentence.

Maytanaya's expression hardened once more as she replied, "Ravan, you seem to forget that I am your wife's elder sister, and I am also your elder sister."

"I have not forgotten, Devi," he countered.

"And Ravan, my heart is entirely devoted to my husband," she asserted.

"Very well, but—"

This 'but' only served to heighten Maytanaya's ire.

"Ravan, you must leave my room at once, or else—"

"Or else what, Devi?" he challenged.

"Or else I will instruct the gaurds to forcibly send you out," she warned.

Ravan remained unfazed, laughing as he stood and approached Maytanaya. "I am utterly enchanted by your extraordinary beauty; I implore you to grant my request."

Maytanaya caught a glimpse of something wickedly in Ravan's gaze. Her expression turned stern as she raised her hands in a commanding gesture, exclaiming, "No."

Yet, Ravan paid no heed to her protest. He began to approach Maytanaya. She retreated, but Ravan advanced, closing the distance between them. As Maytanaya stumbled backward, her hand struck a vessel. She seized it and hurled it at Ravan, who merely laughed and evaded the projectile by leaning to a side.

Maytanaya dashed toward the door, but Ravan seized her clothing and pulled her back. She screamed, yet he grasped her hand, drawing her closer and enveloping her in his arms, kissing her face tenderly.

Luckly at that very moment, Shambar burst in like a tempest. Ravan, taken aback, stepped back, a look of shameless amusement crossing his features. Maytanaya, having escaped Ravan's embrace, rushed to stand beside Shambar, visibly trembling. Her breathing was labored, her face flushed, and her heart raced.

Shambar advanced towards Ravan with great anger. He caught hold of Ravan's hand, almost twisted it and dragged him to a corner of the field outside the palace. Pushed him and made him stand there.

Shambar was going mad with anger, but Ravan did not resist Shambar in any way. He stood in front of Shambar in the field bowing his head before him.

"Ravan, draw your weapon and fight," Shambar commanded.

"No, you may punish me," Ravan replied.

Shambar's voice rose in intensity as he nearly shouted, "Ravan, raise your weapon!"

"No, I will not take up arms; you may punish me," Ravan reiterated.

Furious, Shambar delivered a powerful kick to Ravan. The blow nearly sent him to the ground, but he managed to maintain his balance.

"Don't make excuses Ravan, take up arms and fight", Shambar said.

After this insult, Ravan took up arms. Initially, Ravan avoided attacking Shambar, only dodging his attacks, but after some time he started feeling that Shambar's attacks could kill him. Then he also started attacking Shambar. The war took place and sometimes Shambar overpowered Ravan and sometimes Ravan overpowered Shambar, but finally Ravan was defeated. After beating him hard, Shambar imprisoned him in a dark well.

The entire incident unfolded before Maytanaya like a cinematic experience. She found herself increasingly agitated.

Despite Mayatanya not being at fault in this whole episode, Shambar had distanced himself from her and this had increased Mayatanya's pain a lot. Had Ravan not been the husband of her younger sister, she would have surely got Shambar to punish him with death.

After remembering this episode, Mayatanya once again became very restless. She started feeling as if there was a great heaviness in her chest. She got up and started walking.

Suddenly her foot hit a stone so hard that she fell down. Mayatanya somehow got up and sat there holding her feet, groaning in pain. Once the tears began to flow, Maytanaya felt overwhelmed by her misfortune.

Leaning against the trunk of a tree, she tilted her head back and covered her face with her hands. The tears continued to stream down her cheeks. After wiping her eyes with her fingers, she succumbed to her sorrow.

When she calmed down after a while, she found her throat choked. She ran her hand over her throat and tried to become normal. She felt that she was so tired that she would not be able to walk any more. When she straightened her legs while sitting, she felt as if the pain was coming out of her legs.

Just then she heard a lot of noise outside the palace. Shambar had gone to war, so this noise filled her mind with apprehensions. She hurried toward the palace's main gate.

Outside, a large gathering of mourners had assembled. The noise escalated significantly upon her arrival, causing her heartbeat to quicken and her nerves to heighten. "What has happened?" she inquired.

"Queen, our king has attained martyrdom," a voice came.

"What?" Maytanya's said and with this her face turned pale. She was about to fall when several women rushed to support her.

xxxxxxx

The pyre of Shambar was prepared. The grieving community of Vaijayantpur had gathered at a short distance away. Maytanaya had resolved to become Sati. Calm and composed, she emerged from the palace, followed by a large number of women from the royal household. Memories of her days spent with her father May, her marriage to Shambar, the subsequent events, and the Ravan incident were flooding her mind. She reached the Seete of the cremation. Maytanaya gazed upon the body of Shambar lying on the pyre.

Everything had come to an end. Friendship, enmity, love, and hatred had lost their significance. Suddenly a thought struck her, "And what of Mandodari? Her life has just begun."

'Without Ravan, Mandodari's life will become dark.' Mayatnaya felt that although Ravan's crime was unforgivable, it was a crime committed against her and Shambar. He had already suffered enough punishment by being beaten badly by Shambar and being imprisoned in a blind well for a long time and then Shambar's life was over and her was going to end soon.

She closed her eyes, pressed his lips together slightly, then shook her head slightly and opened her eyes. It appeared from his face as if he had taken a decision. He signaled the servant standing at a distance to come near him. When the servant came,

Maytanaya instructed, "Bring Ravan."

After a while Ravana arrived. Maytanaya was shocked to see Ravana in dirty clothes, with his beard and hair growing unkempt, without shine and without beauty, but the way he was standing showed that he was still not broken. Maytanaya looked at him and turned her face to the other side, then said,

"Free him."

With this, a question arose in her mind whether she was doing something wrong, whether this would give strength to someone's evil intentions, but with this question, the face of her younger sister Mandodari flashed before her eyes once again.

'She had to do this for Mandodari,' she thought. At the same time, she also felt that the heaviness in her chest that she had started feeling some time ago was no longer there.

'Let history interpret this in any way, I have got rid of a big burden before my death,' she thought.

Ravan, upon being extracted from the dark well and learning of Shambar's demise, was initially gripped by the fear that he was being led to his own execution. However, he was taken aback when he was commanded to be released.

He had never dared to hope for such an outcome, even in his wildest dreams. Despite his usual firmness in the face of death, the news of his salvation overwhelmed him. In the realm of warfare, one encounters both victory and defeat, a reality with which Ravan was well acquainted, but today Mayatnaya forgiveness had given him a defeat which he had never faced before. He felt as if Mayatnaya defeating him had moved on to some divine path of victory.

As soon as he was freed from the bondage, Ravan bowed before Mayatnaya.

"Goddess, please do me one more favour", he said to Mayatnaya.

Mayatnaya looked at him in a questioning manner.

"Please don't give up your life", Ravan said.

Mayatnaya did not reply to this. She moved towards Shambar's pyre.

"Can I take the dust from your feet?" Ravan asked.

"There is no need of it", she said and moved ahead.

Ravan stood there and when Mayatnaya reached Shambar's pyre, Ravan closed his eyes. He thought he would not be able to see the scene ahead.

He remained there for a long time with his eyes closed and opened them only when he thought that everything must be over now.

He took the soil from the spot where Maytanaya had stood and spoken to him, applying it to his forehead before departing the cremation ground with deliberate steps and a heavy heart, vowing never to cast an evil eye upon any woman again.

xxxxxxx

The news of Ravan's captivity had reached Mandodari in Lanka, and she was profoundly distressed by it. Mandodari knew that such incidents were not unusual for Ravan; however, she had not anticipated that he would act in such a manner towards her elder sister too. She felt such intense embarrassment that she believed she could not show her face to anyone.

Days passed in untill Mandodari eventually gathered her strength. Perhaps, after such a significant event, Ravan would refrain from casting his gaze upon any other woman. After all, he was her husband. Mandodari began to pray, perform rituals, and observe fasts for Ravan's release, which only intensified with each passing day. As a result, she became increasingly frail and weakened.

And on one fine day, Ravan was there before her, filled with shame and remorse. Mandodari gazed at him, noting his unkempt beard and hair resembling matted locks, and the way he appeared broken, exhausted, and defeated. The Ravan she had once chosen was so different from the one before her now. All her grievances and anger faded away, and as Ravan regained his composure.

"How did all this happen?"Mandodari inquired.

"It was my error," Ravan replied, recounting the events with sincerity and transparency. For a few days, his demeanor was commendable; he appeared composed. However, it was not long before he reverted to his former self.

xxxxxxx

At this point, Sita paused, leaving Ram astonished by the series of events she had just shared.

"Who conveyed this information to you, Mandodari herself?" he asked.

"No, Sarma," Sita responded.

"But did Sarma not betray Mandodari's trust by revealing these details?"

"No, Sarma shared this information only at Mandodari's behest. Mandodari wished for me to understand Ravan's vulnerabilities so that I would not be afraid of him," Sita explained. After a brief silence, she continued,

"I believe Mandodari acted according to her sense of duty, and the love and respect she once held for Ravan had faded from her heart."

xxxxxxx

Sita further narrated,

Ravan had abducted me by deceit during the absence of Lakshman and yourself from Dandakaranya. He took me to his royal palace, showcasing his opulence and narrating tales of his valour and empire. He then proposed that if I agreed to become his queen, he would make all his wives, including Mandodari, my handmaidens.

Mandodari was surprised to see this form of Ravana. She remembered the Ravana who had said that his love knew no boundaries and Mandodari would always have monopoly over it, but then he forgot everything and kept on gathering new beautiful women.

Mandodari also remembered her sister's incident. After which she had thought that now Ravana must have reformed, but now this incident had completely destroyed Mandodari's hope.

During the Surpanakha incident, Mandodari had heard the discussion about you and me and also the talk of Ravana taking revenge for Surpanakha from you and Lakshman, but instead of fighting a man, he chose to torture a woman.This act of Ravan had filled Mandodari with disgust towards him.

"Is deceitfully kidnapping a single woman also bravery?" She had asked Ravana.

"This is diplomacy," Ravan had said.

"Which kind of diplomacy ?"

"He will be very upset and mentally broken due to the loss of his wife, then I will be able to easily conquer him."

"Instead he may become very fierce in anger."

"A person who is angry makes mistakes; his mistakes will also benefit me."

"Even without anger, a person sometimes makes big mistakes."

"What does this mean?" Anger was visible in Ravan's voice.

"How can I say what I want to say, you seem to be angry."

Ravan was irritated. He composed himself and then said,

"What mistake have I done?"

"You should not have kidnapped Sita. Are you not aware of Ram's valour?"

"Why do you doubt my valour?" Ravan said. This statement of Ravan brought to Mandodari's mind the memories of him gathering many women in his inner chambers and then attempting to rape her elder sister and then being beaten by Shambar and being imprisoned in a blind well for a long time.

She laughed sarcastically to herself and then said,

"No, I do not doubt your valour."

Ravan sensed sarcasm in Mandodari's statement and in her tone, but he was not sure. So he did not say anything, but he looked at Mandodari with angry eyes. Mandodari saw Ravan's angry eyes, laughed once again in her mind and said,

"Is the proposal to make Sita your queen also your diplomacy?"

"If Sita accepts this proposal, I will convey this to Ram, he will not be able to bear it, he will break down and I will be able to win over him very easily."

"Do you think Sita will accept it?"

"The fear of life can make one do anything and even if she does not accept it, there is no loss for me."

"And the proposal to make me Sita's maid, what is that?"

"Some temptation has to be given, but don't you trust me?"

"I have seen you, your intelligence, skill and valor all my life. If I don't trust you, then who will?"

Mandodri said, but this time her sarcasm-filled smile could not remain hidden from Ravan. He said angrily,

"No one has the courage to talk to me like this, Mandodari."

"But I have the right to advise you."

"What is your advice?"

"You are neither able to understand the valour of Ram nor the chastity of Sita. Return her with due respect, otherwise I can clearly see the destruction of the entire demon clan," Mandodari said.

"Coward woman," saying this, the angry Ravan left from there stamping his feet. Mandodari understood that Ravan would not understand. He has been subdued by time. Thinking, 'Who knows what else is in fate?' she also left from there.

xxxxxxx

Almost half of the night had passed. The darkness had intensified, and nearly all of Lanka was in sleep, yet Mandodari could not find rest. Exhausted from her restless tossing, she rose and sat up. 'Mandodari was solely concerned about me,' Sita confided to Ram.

'Poor Sita,' Mandodari mused, 'I am uncertain of her current state.' A maid lay sleeping nearby. Mandodari quietly approached her, gently shook her shoulders, and called her name in a hushed tone, "Sarma."

Startled, Sarma awoke and said "Yes plese?"

Mandodari placed a finger on her lips, signaling for silence, and then whispered, "Do you know in which room Sita is being held?"

"No, but I will locate it."

"I must see her without further loss of time."

"Well, I try to manage."

Sarma, being close to Mandodari, understood her distress. "Please wait a moment till I find the appropriate location and return."

"Okay," Mandodari replied.

Sarma got up and left, returning after a short while to inform Mandodari,

"I have located her."

Mandodari approached me and noticed that I was seated on the ground, weeping with my head resting on my knees. She gestured for Sarma to leave and took a seat beside me, calling out, "Seete."

I gradually lifted my head. "Daughter," she had added, "I was surprised by being addressed as 'daughter'," Sita said.

"I am Mandodari, the wife of Ravan."

"What has happened?"

"I wished to see you."

I lacked the courage to ask "why," yet she spoke first, saying, "I can sense your pain."

I remained silent, merely gazing at Mandodari's face.

"I am like a mother to you," she continued.

"But he," I said.

"That Ravan."

I was surprised to hear Mandodari address Ravan in this manner.

"He is very wicked and sinful."

Mandodari's words reduced my tears. I felt some relief, but my deceived mind was still apprehensive. I felt that this could be a trick of Ravan. I still did not say anything. Mandodari understood this.

"Trust me please," she said.

Now I held Mandodari's hand and said in a sad voice

"Mother, please save me."

"Nothing will happen to you, Sita. Just keep your courage. Don't break down."

"Really, mother?"

"Yes, really,"

"I will tell you an incident which will convince you that you need not be afraid of this Ravan."

"Which incident?" I said.

"He is such a sinner that he did not even spare his daughter-in-law."

"Mother, what are you saying?"

"I am telling the truth. Rambha was the wife of Nalakubar, the son of his step brother Kuber. Despite her tears and pleading, he raped her.''

I looked at Mandodari with great surprise at this statement.

"Daughter, you may find this to be unbelievable, but it is really so.''

"How could he do this, mother?'' I asked and then

"I tell you,'' Mandodari said,

"Kumbhinasi is the daughter of Anala, daughter of Malyavan, the elder brother of his maternal grandfather Sumali. A demon named Madhu had forcefully kidnapped her and married her. He became angry on hearing about Kumbhinasi's kidnapping and attacked Madhu with his army.

He was about to kill Madhu in that war when Kumbhinasi came. Crying, she placed her head on his feet and requested him not to make her a widow. He gave Madhu life, but also put a condition that Madhu will have to fight on his behalf in the war with the gods. Madhu agreed.

After this, he attacked Kubera, who was also his step brother and had left the kingdom of Lanka for him and started living on Mount Kailash, and after defeating him, intoxicated with victory, Ravan captured Rambha, the wife of Kubera's son Nalkubar and raped her while torturing her."

Mandodri's words made me feel as if I had seen a gruesome scene. With great difficulty I said,

"Then, mother."

"When Nalakubar came to know about it, he became furious. He challenged Ravan. He wanted to kill him."

"I wish this could happen," I wanted to say, but Ravan is Mandodari's husband, he might feel bad. Thinking this, I stopped.

"Then, did they fight?" I asked.

"No, Ravan is his father's brother, thinking this, Nalakubar stopped. He did not fight with him, but cursed him that if in future he tried to force himself on any woman, his head will be broken into pieces.

"True?" I was filled with surprise and happiness.

"Yes, true and from then till today I have not heard of any rape by him."

"Oh," saying this I breathed a sigh of satisfaction.

"And I feel that by kidnapping you now, he has invited the destruction of the entire demon clan. I don't know what destiny has in mind?" Mandodari said.

"After this, we kept talking to each other till the sound of dawn. Mandodari was filled with sorrow, anger and remorse. She told me many things from the time she met Ravan till today," Sita told Ram.

"Ravan is intelligent, learned and wise, but of crooked mind. He suffers from extreme pride," Mandodari said.

"Mother, how do you live here?" I asked.

"How should I tell you," saying this Mandodari laughed softly and then said that one has to maintain harmony in life."

After this there was silence for a few moments, then

"It is about to dawn, I am leaving, but do not panic and do not lose patience," saying this she stood up to leave, but suddenly as if she remembered something, she added,

"Daughter, Sita,"

"Mother," I said.

"Whenever you meet Ram, convey my regards to him.

saying this Mandodari stroked my head, wiped the tears from my face with her clothes, showered affection on me and then,

"I am leaving, if I get late, the news of meeting you may spread," saying this she quickly left from there.

xxxxxxx

All this is so connected to Sita's memories. People say that if Ravan was not there, Ram would not have been Ram. But what if this Ram or that Ram was not there, but at least Sita would not have to be lost like this,' Ram said to himself.

'From Janakpuri to Sita's departure, 'Sita' is written on every page of my life. Still, those who accuse me of abandoning Sita, who do not even have the courage to stand in front of me, are attacking me from behind.

What kind of people are they for whom even the sacrifice of family and self-interest for the country and society can be a subject of criticism?' Ram thought. He remembered that after telling so much about Mandodari, Sita had paused for a while. Then

'No matter how learned Ravan was, for him a woman was just an object of enjoyment. He had filled his harem with hundreds of women, yet he had tried rape Mandodari's elder sister Mayavati (Maytanya), raped his own daughter-in-law Rambha and then to take revenge on Ram, now he has deceitfully kidnapped his wife.

His pride was sky high. Mandodari was the queen of the royal family, the proposal to make her the slave of a kidnapped woman had pierced his heart like a thorn. So, is it surprising that instead of respect and love, Mandodari developed feelings of anger and hatred for him, even if that person was her husband?

xxxxxxx

Many days had passed since the war in Lanka. First Kumbhakarna and then Meghnad were killed. The news of Meghnad being killed in the war had plunged Lanka into grief. His wife Sulochana had decided to commit sati. Mandodari was already very hurt by this war, then the grief of losing her son Meghnad had made her very restless and now this news of Sulochana's decision to commit sati. She was in great pain. She called Sarma. She was Mandodari's confidant and also intelligent. When Sarma came, Mandodari inquired,

"Sarma, I am hearing that Sulochana has decided to commit sati.

Sarma replied, "Yes, Maharani."

Hearing this Mandodari continued, "Although Meghnad was my son, the thought of a woman perishing in flames alongside a lifeless body strikes me as profoundly inhumane."

Sarma responded, "Indeed, it is inhumane."Mandodari added, "What a horrific and sorrowful sight that would be."

Sarma agreed, "Very much so, yet this is Sulochana's resolve."

"I believe I should attempt to reason with Sulochana."

"Do you think this will yield any positive outcome?" Sarma questioned.

"Perhaps not," Mandodari replied,

"I share the same sentiment, and...," Sarma concurred.

"And what else, Sarma?"

"I fear that your efforts may not convey a favourable message."

"You are correct, yet I would have disregarded such concerns if I could hope that Sulochana might comprehend my intentions," Mandodari agreed with Sarma.

xxxxxxx

Sulochana had indeed become a sati. The conflict with Ram was halted at Ravan's behest following Meghnad's death. Ravan was in a state of deep sorrow and anger. Mandodari approached him, hoping to convey her thoughts once more, but Ravan's agitation was pronounced. Upon seeing her, he declared,

"Mandodari, soon that Ram shall feel the full force of my retaliation."

"You are the last remaining member of this demon lineage. Might you reconsider your course of action before engaging in a direct confrontation with Ram?" Mandodari responded.

"Ravan does not alter his decisions out of fear." Ravan retorted.

"People say he is no ordinary man; he is an incarnation of the divine." Mandodari countered,

"Individuals are free to express their thoughts. Does God truly traverse from one place to another in search of a his partner?" This remark from Ravan deeply wounded Mandodari.

The accounts Mandodari had received about Ram from Sita and

others had instilled a profound respect for him within her. Particularly after witnessing Ravan's true nature, Ram's commitment to monogamy had further elevated her admiration for him.

Mandodari was also pained by Ravan's suggestion to reduce her status to that of Sita's maid. The anguish in her heart manifested in her words.

"No, God would probably change his wife from a queen to a maid for any new woman," Mandodari said in a very low voice. Ravana heard it, but did not reply.

"As long as there is day, a person does not think that night will also come and after that sleeping will be his destiny," she said.

"What is it that you wish to convey, Mandodari?" Ravan's tone turned stern.

"Merely that a person's arrogance often prevents him from acting with due consideration," she replied.

"Mandodari," Ravan nearly shouted, "Do not forget that your status as a royal lady is solely due to my generosity."

"Despite my efforts to forget, I find it impossible. But this moment, I am not your queen, but rather a beneficiary of Sita's grace. Had she accepted your proposal, she would have been the queen, and I would have been relegated to the role of her maid," Mandodari stated with tears in her eyes, pausing to gauge Ravan's reaction.

Her words, along with her piercing gaze, struck Ravan deeply. He glared at her in fury before turning away, muttering, 'Foolish and skeptical woman.'

Following his departure, Mandodari remained in tears for an extended period before finally drying her eyes and reflecting on Ravan's conduct. Throughout his life, he viewed women merely as sources of pleasure. Despite surrounding himself with numerous beautiful women in his palace, his desires were never satisfied. Neither her elder sister Maytanaya nor his daughter-in-law, Rambha, the wife of Kuber's son Nalakuber, could escape his wrath. Although he faced consequences for his actions, he never showed any signs of reform.

As Mandodari recalled Ravan's behaviour, she found herself laughing at her own naivety. Whom was she attempting to persuade? Had Ravan ever heeded anyone's counsel? She remembered how his sister, Suparnakha, was equally independent in her behaviour.

On one occasion, when Mandodari confided in Ravan about her secret meetings with the demon youth Vidyujihva and requested him to discuss this with Suparnakha, he dismissed her concerns. Perhaps Mandodari would not have objected to Suparnakha's association with Vidyujihva, but the situation was complicated by the actions of Vijjala, the mother of Vidyujihva and Mandodari's cousin. Vijjala had fallen in love with another demon. She had brutally murdered her husband, the demon Muchkund, and left his body in a public place. In retaliation, Vidyujihva killed his mother in a fit of rage.

Given Vidyujihva's family background, Mandodari had opposed that relationship. Ravan's indifference to the matter ultimately led to Suparnakha eloping with the demon youth. Enraged, Ravan launched an attack on Vidyujihva with his army, resulting in Vidyujihva's death and leaving Suparnakha a widow.

Seeing her cry, Ravana felt pity. Ravana gave her the region of Dandakaranya and also allowed all the Kalikeya demons from her husband's side to settle in Dandakaranya if they accepted Ravana's Rakshasa-culture, but even after all this, Ravana did not explain to Suparnakha the importance of behaving with restraint as taught by Mandodari leading to her infatuation with Ram and Lakshman, feelings of humiliation, and ultimately, the abduction of Sita.

Mandodari started thinking, 'I tolerated everything silently and accepted it as my fate and even though my love and respect for Ravana may have diminished due to these events, I never let it show in my behaviour, but was it worth tolerating that to take revenge on a man his wife is kidnapped and then I am offered to become her slave? A slave in the same kingdom in which I am living as a queen.' Mandodari felt as if a great pain had risen in her heart.

Resolutely declaring, "I will not weep; I will confront these challenges," Mandodari shook her head and rose to her feet. She resolved to thwart Ravan's intentions and protect Sita.

"This daughter of the demon May is a royal queen and shall forever remain so," Mandodari affirmed to herself.

Continued to walk
Among the thorny path
Bleeding wounds
And persisting pain
Still maintaining the composure
Yet somewhere inside
A rebellion emerged

Sita concluded her narrative and turned to Ram, who was listening to everything very seriously. Once she finished, he remarked,

"Oh, now it is evident why Mandodari agreed to become Vibhishana's queen fafter Ravan's demise."

9.
On the River Bank

Ram cherished playing the veena by the banks of the Saryu River during the evenings, enjoying the serene flow of the water or taking leisurely strolls along the shore. Whenever time permitted, he and Sita would visit the riverbank together.

On one such occasion, their chariot halted at the Saryu's edge. Ram gestured for the charioteer to stop, and they made their way to the water. Upon reaching the bank, Sita dipped her fingers into the river, splashing water playfully towards Ram. The droplets landed on his face, prompting laughter between them. As he wiped the water away, he teased,

"Isn't childhood over yet?"

"Why should it be?" Sita said laughing.

"Yes, this is also right, why should it go?" Saying this, Ram also laughed and he also filled his palm with river water to pour on Sita. Now Sita playfully grasped Ram's hand and splashed the water back at him. And then they settled down by the riverbank.

Ram's gaze was fixed on the river's current. Noticing this, Sita inquired, "What has captured your attention?"

"Nothing, Sita, it just occurred to me that I have been seeing this river since my childhood, I don't know how much water must have flowed since then, but the river is still the same."

"You tend to become philosophical quite early," Sita remarked but "I have no desire to be a philosopher." With that, she walked a short distance along the riverbank, leaving Ram standing alone. After a moment, Sita glanced back, only to find Ram still focused on the river. Seizing the opportunity for some mischief, she concealed herself behind a large tree and kept watching Ram.

After a while, when Ram noticed Sita's absence he began to search for her. Growing increasingly anxious, he called out, "Sita."

Seeing Ram's distress, Sita burst into laughter and she emerged from her hiding spot.

"Where were you hiding? I was quite frightened," Ram admitted.

"Why were you frightened? I was right here," Sita replied.

"Once, you were away from me for thirteen months, and after a lot of struggle, I was able to find you. Now I don't want to lose you even for a moment."

"Is that so?" Sita asked, "Then will you please tell me one thing?"

"Yes, why not?"

"What were your thoughts when you returned from hunting the golden deer and found that I was not there?"

"I was taken aback. Initially, I thought you might have wandered off for some reason, but soon I began to sense that you were in some sort of trouble."

"We were living there for a long time, then when I was not seen for some time, the thought of me being in trouble came to your mind, nothing else, why?"

"I cannot tell this, but some anxiety definitely arose in my mind due to your absence."

"Our minds are interconnected," Sita remarked, a faint smile accompanied by a hint of shyness gracing her features. After a brief pause, she continued, "Perhaps this is the bond that unites us."

Ram chuckled and replied, "Regardless of what binds us, we are one."

A subtle blush crept across Sita's cheeks as she inquired, "Well when you could not trace me then?"

"We became very much worried about you and started searching you vehemently, but upon encountering Jatayu, everything became clear."

"Then?"

"I felt as though blood had surged into eyes of both Lakshman and myself."

"Oh," saying this, Sita held Ram's hand in her hands, pressed it and then put it on her forehead as if someone was expressing his gratitude. There was silence for some time, then Sita broke the silence,

"May I ask you one more thing?"

"What?"

"People say that you killed Bali by deceit."

"Bali was a wicked man, a friend of Ravan and also a protector of Ravan's interests in that region. His killing was the first step towards Ravan's destruction."

"But killing by deceit," Sita said.

"Is this worth considering when it comes to fighting the evil?"

Sita became silent at this. She did not find anything worth protesting. After some time she said,

"Shall we go near the river?"

"Yes please come", saying this Ram stood up. Sita got up and plucked some flowers from a plant planted at some distance and kept them in her aanchal (a part of ladies' clothing). Then they went to the bank of the river and stood walking in water up to their ankles.

Sita started putting the flowers in Saryu. Both of them were watching the flowers float in the water like children. After floating all the flowers in the water, Sita shook her aanchal and said laughingly,

"Finished."

"What?"

"Flowers with me."

"Your aanchal will never be empty of flowers, Sita."

"Yes, since you are in my aanchal," saying this Sita laughed again. Ram also laughed at this and then said,

"Sita, you say that you are the daughter of the earth."

"Yes, I have heard this since childhood."

"And sometimes I feel that I, who have grown up drinking the water of this Saryu, am the son of Saryu," said Ram.

"Sita, I feel that as this river has moved ahead taking the flowers from your Aanchal, similarly… Ram further added.

"Similarly what?"

"May flowers always keep falling from your Aanchal and may my life keep flowing like the flow of a river, gathering them."

"Shall I tell you what I feel?" Sita said.

"Yes Sita, please, I want to know your sentiments."

"To me, you seem like this sky, whose vastness has no limits, and…."

"And?"

"And may flowers flourish beneath this sky, and may the Anchal of this earth's daughter always be adorned with them," Sita remarked. After a brief pause, she added playfully, "Are we composing a song?" Ram laughed and replied,

"No, perhaps we are living the song."

"How so?" Sita inquired.

"Consider this, Sita: do our emotions not seem to breathe? The essence of beauty has transitioned from our eyes to our hearts, and there is an artistic quality in our expressions. Ultimately, it is all one song."

With a smile, Sita responded affirmatively, holding Ram's hand.

"Did you enjoy my song?" Ram asked.

"Very much," Sita replied, gently touching Ram's fingers to her eyes and reiterating, "I truly liked this song."

"Sita, I feel that if a beautiful song could have a body, it would be very much like you."

Sita laughed. Ram pointed towards the sky and continued,

"Sita, I sense that this sky and this earth are abundant with blessings for us."

"It is indeed our good fortune," Sita acknowledged. Ram grasped Sita's hand and proposed, "Shall we return?"

"No, let us sit a little longer. You did bring the veena, did you not?" Sita asked.

"Yes, it is on the chariot."

"Will you not play it for a while?"

"Okay," saying this Ram got up and signaled the charioteer standing a little away. When he came near Ram asked him to bring the Veena. When the Veena came Ram sat down with it on the bank of the river.

Sita also came and sat nearby. They did not know for how long they were lost in the tunes of the Veena, but when darkness started to set in Sita herself said to Ram,

"Shall we leave?"

By the time they reached the palace, evening had descended, and the lamps were aglow. They were being awaited in the palace.

"We are late," Sita remarked.

"Yes, our conversation had become a little too long."

"But it was very nice. If we get time, we will go again tomorrow," Sita said.

"Okay," Ram said and then both of them got busy with their daily chores.

xxxxxxx

The following evening, as dusk approached, Sita arrived.

"Shall we go?" She asked smilingly.

Sensing that her laughter radiated from her eyes as well as her lips.

"Are you interested in going?" Ram asked.

"Yes, if you are available."

"Do you wish to pose another question today?" he inquired.

Feeling a bit bashful. "How did you perceive that?" she responded.

"I am seeing it's reflection in your eyes."

Sita replied with a laugh.

"So, we are going, correct?" she added.

With a simple "Yes," Ram moved ahead.

"Will you not take Veena?" she asked.

"Of course, I will."

Sita asked a maid to bring Ram's Veena and taking it from her she accompanied Ram. They came out of the palace, the chariot was almost ready. They sat in the chariot and got down after reaching the river. They left the chariot and started walking towards the bank.

"Would you prefer to walk or sit somewhere?" Ram inquired.

"Let us walk," she replied.

"Alright."

After a brief period of silence, Sita spoke up, "Yesterday, I posed a question to you."

"Indeed, you had asked that how I had felt upon returning after slaying the golden deer and finding you missing."

"I have another question in my mind."

"What is that?" he asked.

"After my abduction, you must have required allies, first to locate me and then to confront Ravan."

"Indeed, allies were essential, and that almighty ensured their availability. Jatayu, Hanuman, Sugriva, Jamvant, and later Vibhishana—divine assistance had brought forth numerous supporters."

"It is appropriate to express gratitude to God, as all occurrences are a result of His grace; however, you could have sought assistance from Ayodhya or Mithila as well."

"Indeed, Sita, this notion had crossed my mind for a while, but I ultimately dismissed it."

"Why so?"

"Sita, think that if this news had reached the common people of Ayodhya or Mithila that you are missing, who knows what kind of reactions would have been there," Ram said.

"But after knowing my where abouts?" Sita asked.

"Lakshman was by my side, and we had confidence in our strength."

Ram paused momentarily before continuing,

"And what about you?"

"What do you mean?"

"Do you not have faith in my strength?"

Sita grasped Ram's arm and rested her head against it, saying, "I possess immense and unwavering faith."

"Remember, Sita, your Ram has never sought anything from anyone."

"I am aware," Sita replied.

"Like others, I have experienced both joy and sorrow, yet they have not troubled me thus far."

What could Sita say, she kept looking at Ram's face for some time, then closed her eyes. After some time

Ram called out, "Sita."

"Yes," Sita opened her eyes.

"What are you thinking?"

"I am thinking, how great is the fortune of getting you, and how small is my Aanchal."

"You love me deeply, don't you, Sita?"

"How do you feel?"

"I do feel it?"

"Then why are you asking?"

"I do not think that it is a great fortune to get me and your Aanchal is not small but very big, Sita."

"Well how big is my Aanchal?"

Ram looked towards the sky and said, "The whole sky can be adjusted in your Anchal."

Sita loughed at it.

"I feel like saying something Sita."

"Yes please."

"I feel that beauty is God's musical creation and is above definitions."

"Yes, and look, no one has control over the dreams of sleeping eyes, but the dreams of awake eyes must be beautiful."

Sita offered a slight smile in response to Ram's remark, then pursed her lips, widened her gaze, shook her head, and thoughtfully uttered a prolonged "Hum..." before adding, "I believe there exists a dream within your eyes as well."

"Indeed, there is a remarkably beautiful dream residing in my eyes too," he replied.

"Okay! What is the dream of your eyes?" Sita said mischievously while laughing. Ram laughed and said,

"There is you and only you,"

Sita laughed again and said,

"My good fortune," and then she closed her eyes as if she had achieved so much that there was nothing left to achieve.

And then for a long time they remained immersed in the tunes of the Veena.

10.
Another Deepawali

Days don't stop. Diwali had come again. Another anniversary of the return of Ram, Sita and Lakshman from exile. Every year on this day, after the worship of Lakshmi-Ganesh in the evening, rows of lamps were decorated in the houses and people used to celebrate that event for many days.

Although Deepawali had come again, but Sita was not there, there were no celebrations and the whole Ayodhya seemed sad.

Manas and Chitra had completed the puja, but a sense of restlessness lingered. Manas stepped outside and stood in contemplation. After a while, Chitra joined him, and they began to wander aimlessly. Eventually, Chitra remarked, "I feel compelled to visit the place where Mother's footprints were discovered."

"I was thinking the same," Manas replied.

"It is evening now, and it will be dark by the time we return. Should we take something to illuminate our path?" Chitra suggested.

As Manas and Chitra commenced their journey, darkness gradually enveloped the surroundings. Mans shielded the lamp he had brought along, ignited it, and proceeded forward, guided by its glow. He made concerted efforts to protect the flame from being extinguished by the gusts of wind. The path through the forest was fraught with obstacles, thorns, and the sounds of wildlife, yet his resolve remained unshaken, and fear did not take hold of him. It felt as though he was being driven by an unseen force.

Eventually, they arrived at the grove of trees where Sita's footprints had been discovered at the time of her departure. There were proposals to develop the area, construct a road leading to it, erect an idol of Sita Ji, and establish a temple in her honour. However, when this suggestion was presented to Ram, he rejected it.

He could not agree to belittle Sita's sacrifice and renunciation by making her a goddess. Also, he did not want to destroy the naturalness of that place. He wanted to preserve everything related to Sita as it was. Then, as per Ram's wish, that place was fenced all around and protected from animals and left as it was.

How many thorns must have pricked Sita's feet while going there, what must have been the condition of her feet, Ram wanted to keep that experience alive too, so the path leading to that place was left after repairing it a little.

Manas and Chitra reached that place and put the lamp they had brought with them on the ground, bowed their heads on the ground and sat there with folded hands. There was silence all around. Chitra broke the silence,

"Did you notice one thing?"

"What?"

"We came from home to here and despite the winds on the way, our lamp kept burning, it did not go off even once."

"Yes, it is surprising."

"Moreover, even in this open space, it is burning steadily."

"Indeed, and the fragrance here is delightful as well."

"Yes, really," said Chitra.

"And look at the light spread here, such a small lamp and so much light.

This light cannot be only the light of this lamp, Chitra."

"True."

"Chitra, your voice is very good, why don't you sing some praise of God," said Manas.

"Alright," Chitra replied, and she began to sing praises to God. The atmosphere was filled with music as her voice resonated in the surroundings. Manas listened quietly, his eyes closed, occasionally joining in on certain lines.

Chitra seemed to recall numerous hymns, continuing to sing one after another, unaware of how much time had elapsed. By the time she concluded her praises, it was already quite late.

Just then, they sensed someone approaching from behind. Upon turning, they were taken aback to find a person standing there, holding a lamp and flowers. Manas and Chitra stepped aside as the individual placed the lamp down, offered the flowers, folded his hands, and then bowed his head to the ground. After a while, when he lifted his head, Manas and Chitra noticed tears in his eyes. This was the same individual who had initially doubted Sita and had been leading a group of such people.

His expression revealed that he had wept extensively. Manas and Chitra perceived that the tears in his eyes were those of remorse. They felt it would be best to give him space to express the sorrow he had been harboring.

They looked at each other and then, Manas said,

"Let's leave."

"Yes."

"And Deepak?"

"Let's leave Deepak here. Will this place of Maa remain dark?"

"Then how will we see the way?"

"Let us proceed, keeping mother in our thoughts. She will show us the way."

"Okay, let's leave."

Manas and Chitra left the lamp behind and ventured out into that moonless night. However, as they exited that location, they noticed someone ahead on the path to their home, carrying a lamp. They speculated that it might be a traveler like themselves and decided to follow him for safety.

Upon returning home, Manas and Chitra observed a large group of people gathered in one area, engaged in discussion. They joined the assembly and learned that everyone had come to pay their respects at Sita's departure Seete.

"Oh! It is good that we have already viSeeted that place, otherwise, we may have been deprived of those wonderful and divine experiences that we had,"Manas said, and with a sense of reverence.

They continued to watch the groups moving toward their destination one after another, and then after some time Manas and Chitra set off toward their home.

xxxxxxx

The day passed quietly within the palace. The Lakshmi puja had been conducted, yet it appeared as if it was a mere formality. There was a lack of enthusiasm. After worshipping Laxmi, everyone sat together for some time, then Ram stood up and the others also followed him.

Ram walked from there and came out of the palace. Lakshman was following him. He asked,

"Are you heading somewhere?"

"Yes, to Sita's resting place."

"Resting place?" Lakshman had always referred to that location as 'Prayana-sthal, i.e. 'place of departure. So he was somewhat taken aback by Ram's use of the term 'resting place.'

"Indeed, Sita must have found her final rest there," Ram replied.

Lakshman fell silent after responding with a simple "yes."

The mention of Sita's death made Lakshman feel a strange suffocation in his heart. He pressed his lips. His eyes were moist.

When Ram saw this he said,

"Lakshman, I can see that your eyes are moist, but though Sita's body is not among us, she is immortal, and no one can kill her."

Lakshman listened to it quietly. He did not say anything even after this. Ram said again,

"Sita possessed a remarkable character, Lakshman, and her heart was tender. There can be no doubt regarding her integrity, despite the foolish inquiries some had made. I believe that Sita, who exhibited immense patience and purity akin to the sacred Ganges, must have felt excruciating pain at the accusations against her character, leading her to choose to depart from this world."

Lakshman continued to listen in silence. Ram, overtaken by emotion, added,

"Laxman, while leaving the Ashwamedha Yagya Seete, she had looked at me. There was a sea of pain in her eyes and a slight smile on her lips. I can understand the matter of the eyes, but I wonder how deep her pain must have been when a smile must have appeared on her lips," saying this Ram became silent. It seemed as if he was lost somewhere.

"It is also possible Lakshman, that so that I do not break down, she might have looked at me with the tears in her eyes and a smile on her lips, but the pain visible on her face could not be hidden.

I will forever remember those eyes and that smile," Ram said, taking a deep breath before pausing again.

"At times, life is merely a series of adjustments," he continued. "And there are moments when fatigue sets in during a long journey, making it immensely comforting to close one's eyes and rest quietly."

"Lakshman, one very good thing about life is death," Ram added.

Lakshman who was listening to Ram very quietly and seriously said,

"Brother, can I say something?"

"Yes Lakshman, say it."

"Bhabhi was very nice, it is impossible to forget her, but who has been able to hold the rays in hands, they come, give light and go away. Take care of yourself brother."

Ram's eyes were wet, yet he laughed and said,

"You are right Lakshman, I was drowning in philosophy."

After this there were wet eyes on both sides. No one spoke anything for some time, then Lakshman broke the silence,

"The mothers and Urmila also wanted to go."

"Okay Lakshman, you bring them in the chariot."

"And you?"

"I prefer to walk to that place; after all, Sita also traveled there on foot."

"Brother, if you will walk, no one will take the chariot, not even the mothers. Will they be able to manage such a long journey on foot?"

"Even if they could, it would not be fitting. Alright, Lakshman, summon anyone who wishes to join us; we shall travel only by chariot."

Lakshman went inside to relay the message, and soon the entire royal family emerged, ready to depart. Manthara followed Kaikeyi, standing aside with hesitation. She wished to join but found it difficult to express. Ram noticed her and, understanding her unspoken desire, asked, "Do you want to come?"

She lowered her head in response.

"Come and take a seat in the chariot," Ram encouraged.

Manthara hesitantly climbed into the mothers' chariot.

They reached in a short while, the place where Sita had left came.

Everyone got down from the chariot and went near that tree, bowed down and stood there.

Kaikeyi lit a lamp there and others paid their respects by offering flowers.

Lav and Kush sat there after bowing to that land.

"Sitting here, I feel as if we are sitting in the lap of our mother," said Luv.

"I feel the same, Luv," replied Kush.

The flickering light of the lamps burning there in the darkness of the no moon night, the fragrance of the many flowers placed there and the feeling of a halo, altogether being there felt like being immersed in sanctity.

Everyone stood there for some time, immersed in the experience of that sanctity. No one wanted to return from there, but there was a continuous stream of visitors and the crowd was increasing, so they decided to return. Luv and Kush again put their heads on the ground, applied the soil from there on their foreheads and stood up.

After this, everyone returned. No one spoke anything throughout the journey, only the sound of a woman's sobs was breaking the silence in between.

xxxxxxx

After returning to the palace, everyone once again gathered at the place of worship.

The lamp dedicated to Lakshmi ji flickered, prompting Kaushalya to instruct her daughters-in-law to replenish it with ghee, ensuring it would burn throughout the night. She then proposed,

"Come, let us all go to Sita's room. The lamps will be lit there first." Everyone started walking towards Sita's room with Kaushalya. No changes had been made there since Sita had left. Very often Ram used to go and sit there for some time.

Urmila, Mandvi, and Shrutikirti positioned lamps around the room and ignited them.

"Ensure that every room and corner of the palace is illuminated," Kaushalya instructed her daughters-in-law.

As they began to leave, Ram hesitated, seemingly reluctant to depart so soon. Kaushalya, observing Ram's demeanor, understood his feelings and discreetly signaled for everyone except him to exit.

Once alone, Ram remained in Sita's room for a while, absorbing the familiar surroundings. He eventually sat down, his gaze fixed on Sita's portrait, and after a moment, he closed his eyes. In a brief span, he lost awareness of his physical form, feeling as though Sita was present within and around him, enveloping him entirely.

Upon the return of the daughters-in-law, who had been admiring the arrangement of lamps throughout the palace, Kaushalya instructed them to prepare a meal for everyone. Traditionally, the women would only begin their meal after the men had finished, but on this occasion, Kaushalya decided that the entire family would dine together. However, Ram had not yet arrived.

Lakshman took it upon himself to bring Ram. Upon reaching Sita's chamber, he found Ram seated with his eyes closed, seemingly lost in thoughts. Lakshman stood quietly, awaiting the moment Ram would open his eyes.

Though Ram's eyes were closed, he appeared to sense this presence and eventually opened his eyes. Seeing Ram awake, Lakshman gently called out to him.Ram turned his gaze towards him.

"Everyone is waiting for you at dinner," Lakshman informed him.

"Oh," Ram replied, rising to his feet.

It was the festival of Diwali, and a variety of dishes had been prepared; however, none partook of the meal with enthusiasm. The dinner concluded in a hushed atmosphere, and soon after, everyone quietly retreated to his respective room.

xxxxxxx

As Ram entered his own room, a knock sounded at the door. He opened it to find Kaikeyi standing there.

"Come in Mother,please," Ram invited her with due respect. Kaikeyi entered. She appeared very sad. At Ram's request she took a seat.

"Mother, you appear very sad," Ram said.

Kaikeyi was sitting with her head bowed down. On hearing Ram's question, she raised her head once and looked at him and then started looking into the void somewhere above. Ram again said,

"Mother, what troubles you? You seem very sorrowful."

"My son, I never anticipated that my minor misjudgment would lead to such significant repercussions. I feel like a criminal, and the weight of my guilt is unbearable," she confessed.

"Mother, even if you have erred, the suffering you have endured is not insignificant," Ram reassured her.

"You have risked your life twice to save our father's, and if you view my exile as a fateful event only, then throughout your life, you have shown me more affection than Bharat. Everyone is aware of this. My respect for you is equal to that which I hold for Mata Kaushalya."

Kaikeyi's heart was already filled with pain. Ram's sympathetic words made her cry.

"Your weeping is hurting me a lot mother and I also feel that I have committed some mistake in your respect."

Concerned, Ram approached her closely and took her hand in his hands. Subsequently, Kaikeyi rose, embraced Ram, and gently stroked him before pulling away to say, "No, Ram, you and Sita have always shown me immense respect and love."

"Then, please, release yourself from this guilt, Mother."

Kaikeyi responded, "Very well," and settled back down. Although her sobbing had diminished, it had not entirely ceased. Ram sat beside her, resting his hand on her head and allowing her to lean on his shoulder. After a while, Kaikeyi's tears subsided. She stood, dried her tear-streaked face with a cloth, and said, "I am leaving."

"Very well, Mother, but please take care of yourself," Ram replied.

Kaikeyi exited the room slowly, while Ram observed her departure. He recalled that upon their return from the forest after fourteen years, she had been the most joyful. Kaikeyi had embraced him, Sita, and Lakshman in succession, celebrating their return with great enthusiasm. She had busied herself throughout the night, ensuring that the lamps in the palace remained lit.

When Lakshman had touched her feet, she had grasped his hands and said, "Lakshman, I have heard that you are very upset with me. Will you please not forgive your mother?"

"Mother, that time has passed; I am your son, and you are still my mother," Lakshman had replied.

She then led Sita to her chamber, saying, "Daughter, I had sent you wearing bark clothes. I have already received the punishment for that sin. I have lost my husband and Bharat also does not address me as a mother. Will you call me Mother?"

"Mother, you are always my mother," Sita said to her.

As soon as Sita's words resonated in Ram's mind, a cascade of memories from that day and their shared past flooded his thoughts.

Sita's face always radiated glow, and on that particular day of Ashvamedha ceremony, she was no exception, her glow had intensified after the event, when she bid farewell to everyone.

Kaikeyi's maid Manthara was very scared after Ram returned from the forest, but Sita was also concerned about her. Manthara felt that perhaps Lakshman would punish her, so as soon as Sita got a chance, she called her and assured her that there was no need to be afraid.

Despite days full of very busy activities, Sita also took care of her, which had become the initial reason for her going into exile.

xxxxxxx

Ever since Sita had gone, Ram had increased his busy schedule, but still, he was unable to escape her memories. As soon as he got some solitude, Sita's memories would surround him, and today was a special day. He was lost in Sita's memories when he was startled by mother Kaushalya's voice.

"Ram," it was Kaushalya's voice.

"Yes," saying this Ram raised his head, and seeing Kaushalya in front of him he was a little surprised and also felt embarrassed about his state of mind due to which he could not notice her arrival.

"Mother, when did you arrive?" he inquired.

"Just now," she replied.

"Please, have a seat."

"Yes, I will," she affirmed.

Kaushalya not only took a seat but also asked Ram to sit beside her, holding his hand. Like a nurturing mother, she placed her hand on his forehead and began to comb his hair. After a brief silence, she remarked, "You seem very sad."

"No, Mother, I have learned to endure challenging circumstances," he responded.

"I understand," Kaushalya acknowledged, pausing momentarily before continuing, "Every year on this occasion, King Janak used to visit us or send a message, but this time, nothing is there."

"His message has arrived, Mother. He has expressed that the mere thought of Ayodhya's desolation in Sita's absence brings him great sorrow. Consequently, he has decided not to visit Ayodhya, as the pain of her absence would be too much for him to bear. However, he has sent his warm regards along with numerous gifts,"Ram said.

"Ram, I am not surprised that King Janaka, who is also known as Videha, is so upset due to Sita's absence.I am surprised at how he must have endured the pain of his daughter's departure in this manner."

Ram remained silent.

"It is getting late; I shall take my leave, and you should also rest," Kaushalya remarked. As she began to rise, Ram gently held her back and urged her not to leave.

"Please mother don't leave me alone," he requested.

Kaushalya laughed softly, "Very well," she replied, and settled down beside him. Ram lay close to her, resting his head against her. Kaushalya tenderly placed her hand on his head, running her fingers through his hair. After a while, Ram adjusted his position and fell asleep with his mother's head nestled against his chest.

xxxxxxx

Ram fell asleep, but Kaushalya could not. After some time, she slowly removed her head from Ram's chest, brought her head to par with Ram's head, and started looking at his face.

While sleeping, Ram's hair fell on his forehead and face. Kaushalya gently moved Ram's hair back and caressed his face and then started caressing his head slowly saying 'my child'. How small he was when he went with his younger brother Lakshman to kill Tadaka and other demons on the insistence of sage Vishwamitra, she thought.

She remembered how King Dasharath himself had become very upset when Vishwamitra had asked him to send Ram and Lakshman to his ashram to kill these demons. Initially, he was not ready for it but when Vishwamitra and Guru Vashishtha convinced him, he agreed to send Ram and Lakshman to Vishwamitra's ashram.

Kaushalya also remembered how Kaikeyi had wept bitterly after this and how she and Sumitra had endured this separation from their children with a heavy heart.

When Kaushalya's flow of thoughts broke, she looked at Ram's face. He was sleeping soundly like a tired child.

Kaushalya again started caressing his face and hair like a small child, then after some time she lifted Ram's hand, bent it and started looking at it by entangling her fingers in his.

'How many great demons has my child destroyed with these soft hands?' saying this Kaushalya placed Ram's fingers on her eyelids, then kissed his palm and lay down pressing that hand to her chest.

She felt very tired. Perhaps it was because of the day's running around, she thought, but she was unable to sleep. With Ram's palm pressed to her chest, she again got lost in thoughts.

xxxxxxx

Ram, Sita and Lakshman had left for the forest. Sadness and silence had spread throughout Ayodhya. People were busy with their work but the smile on their faces had vanished. Ram's departure to the forest was a topic of discussion in the houses, streets and squares of the city.

hile the citizens praised Sita and Lakshman, their ire was directed towards Kaikeyi. The two boons granted by King Dasharatha were perceived as a curse by the people of Ayodhya, and Kaikeyi's actions were widely condemned. Public opinion regarding King Dasharatha was divided; some viewed his decision as a necessary obligation due to his promise, while others were critical of him.

There was a lot of discussion among the people about how Bharat would take this on his return from his maternal home and those who knew Bharat's love for Ram were sure that Bharat would be sorrowful on hearing these things.

The discussion among the common people was reaching the palace. Kaikeyi also had the same apprehension as the public sentiment were towards Bharat. She was very much looking forward to Bharat's arrival and knowing his reaction. If Bharat happily accepted the kingship then it was fine otherwise Kaikeyi thought that she would try to convince him, but in some corner of her mind, she also thought that what if Bharat did not agree? This 'if' had made Kaikeyi very restless, and in every glance that looked towards her in the entire palace, Kaikeyi saw only the feeling of contempt towards her. She had confined herself to her private room.

King Dasharath had become very sad, unwell and weak. Tears were not stopping from his eyes. Kaushalya and Sumitra too had many complaints against King Dasharath, but on seeing their condition they forgot their sorrows.

Kaushalya brought him to her palace so that they could be taken better care of. Dasharath saw Kaushalya's concern for him,

"You are worried for no reason Kaushalya, I will not survive, and without Ram I don't find any meaning in my life," he said to Kaushalya.

"I also don't find any meaning in life without Ram, but he has gone only for fourteen years, this time too will pass," Kaushalya said.

"I will not be able to wait for fourteen years, Kaushalya, I am in a hurry."

Kaushalya put her palm on Dasharath's mouth,

"What are you saying?" he said.

Dasharath very softly removed Kaushalya's hand from his mouth. "Let me say it Kaushalya, don't stop me."

"Firstly you get well, then tell all these things. Once you get well, we will go to the forest to meet our children. There is no restriction on this."

"You can definitely go to meet them, but I don't have time, so let me say whatever I want to ,"

After this Kaushalya became silent and started looking at Dasharath's face.

"Kaushalya, you are elder, please forgive Kaikeyi, she is not as much at fault as it is being perceived."

Kaushalya did not understand this and did not like it either, she looked at Dashrath with questioning eyes.

"My own mistakes are more responsible for all this," Dashrath said.

"I could not understand you."

"I was responsible for Shrvan kumar's death. I had shot that arrow only after hearing the sound, which took the life of Shravan Kumar, the only support of his blind parents whereas before shooting an arrow at anyone, we must ensure who our target is.

Taking the life of an innocent is not a small mistake and then if the sigh of the blind, helpless and old Shravan's parents or any helpless person who is harassed without any reason goes in vain, then won't people lose faith in God?"

What could Kaushalya say on it, she observed silence.

"I am sure that I am facing this situation because of that sin. And as far as Kaikeyi is concerned, she has saved my life once during the war with Shambar and next time during a life-threatening illness by putting her own life in danger. I have never forgotten this, but because of Kaikeyi, not only Ram, Sita and Lakshman but also the people of Ayodhya have suffered a lot.

This is extremely painful and then sending Sita to the forest in just bark clothes is also extremely condemnable."

After saying this, Dasharatha fell silent, gazing at Kaushalya's face, perhaps anticipating a response. However, Kaushalya remained unresponsive. Observing Dasharatha's growing fatigue from the lengthy discourse, she gently remarked,

"You appear weary from speaking for so long. We can address the remaining matters later."

"No, Kausalya, allow me to continue; I'm not sure I'll get another chance to say all this."

At this, Kaushalya refrained from further comment, instead, she placed her hand tenderly on Dasharatha's hand.

Dasharath took Kaushalya's hand between his palms and said,

"There is one more thing Kaushalya."

"What is that?"

The issue of my granting two boons to Kaikeyi has become a topic of discussion; however, it is important to recall that during the time when you and Sumitra were childless, I had sought Kaikeyi's hand from her father with the hope of having a child. At that moment, prior to this marriage, her father had extracted a promise from me that only the son born to Kaikeyi would inherit the throne of Ayodhya. I had indeed made that promise, Kaushalya.

"We had no objections to Bharat ascending the throne, but what necessitated Ram's exile?" Kaushalya inquired.

"Perhaps Kaikeyi feared that Bharat might face challenges in ruling alongside a highly capable elder brother," was the response.

"What challenges? Could Ram ever harbour ill thoughts towards Bharat?" she questioned.

The reply came, "Not at all, yet the possibility of public discontent cannot be ruled out."

"Indeed, that possibility can not be ruled out," she acknowledged.

"Besides this Kausalya, there may be some benefits hidden in this episode. These may be some social interests in Ram going to the forest," he addedd.

"Therefore, Kausalya, I urge you not only to forgive Kaikeyi but also, as being the eldest in this house after my departure, to encourage others to let go of their grievances against her," he pleaded.

Kausalya remained silent and thoughtful.

"Promise me, Kaushalya, that you will do this. Bitterness among family members is always destructive," Dasharatha insisted.

She replied, "I assure you that I will pay attention to your points and ensure that these will not be disregarded."

Exhausted from this lengthy conversation, Dasharatha took Kaushalya's hand, holding it close to his heart.

"I have very little time left," he said and with these words, his head tilted to one side. Kaushalya just kept looking with sadness and surprise. Dashrath had gone.

Son and daughter-in-law, in exile for fourteen years and on the way to Dandakaranya had already given her unbearable pain, and now the husband's death in this manner. All this was like a terrible thunderbolt for Kaushalya. Kaushalya started weeping loudly. Sumitra was somewhere nearby. She also came. Daughters-in-law Urmila, Mandavi and Shrutikirti also came. In a short while the entire palace gathered there.

Kaikeyi was in her room. When she heard the cries of Kaushalya and Sumitra, she understood that King Dasharath was no more. She knew that they were very sad in grief for their son, but she had thought that everything would be fine after a few days. She had not feared such an unfortunate incident so soon.

Kaikeyi's heart trembled. She was sad about King Dasharath's death, but she was afraid of people's reactions if she went out. Manthara was standing nearby. Kaikeyi looked at her. There was fear in her eyes too.

Kaikeyi asked her to go out and find out the real thing. Manthara went but returned very quickly. Their fear was true. The king had died. The fear of public condemnation and confusion also appeared in Kaikeyi's eyes.

"What should we do?" Kaikeyi asked Manthara.

"Let's go there," Manthara said.

"I am afraid that people will react to us and I don't know what kind of reactions they will give."

"We have to go there anyway, otherwise those reactions will be more intense. Also, with Maharaja no more, there is no obstacle left in Bharat becoming the king. He will be coming. After that you will be the queen mother, so I don't think anyone will dare to say anything in front of you."

"I don't know about that, but yes, we have to go," saying this Kaikeyi got up and, somewhat apprehensive and somewhat scared, reached Kaushalya's palace, where the dead body of King Dasharath was lying, and started crying.

No one said anything to Kaikeyi, nor did anyone talk to her, but Kaikeyi clearly saw the feelings of neglect and anger towards her in the eyes of the women present there. While crying, Kaushalya's eyes went towards Kaikeyi. For a moment, Kaushalya forgot to cry, she felt as if her misfortune was standing in front of her in person, but then she remembered Dashrath's words. She held Kaikeyi's hand and brought her closer.

Kaikeyi, who was afraid that she might have to face humiliation, was a little surprised by Kaushalya's behaviour and saying

"Didi, it is because of me that we have to see this day," she hugged Kaushalya and started crying.

"Don't say this Kaikeyi, maybe this was written in our fate," Kaushalya said, but her pain and grief were unbearable, then Sumitra came forward and held her.

"Didi, we have to fight the circumstances, what has happened cannot be changed, but these days that have come in our life like a night will also pass," Sumitra said.

xxxxxxx

As Kaushalya lay on the bed, her fingers gently caressing Ram's head, she felt as though the events were unfolding before her once more.

Suddenly, her thoughts shifted, and the image of Sita during the Ashwamedha Yagya came to her mind. She recalled that after Sita's departure, people had proclaimed her to be a goddess, and she had seemingly vanished into the earth.

She was indeed a goddess," Kausalya said to herself. It was late in the night. There was a deep silence all around. In the light of the dim lamp burning in the room, she looked at the picture of Sita hanging on the wall.

Sita's face seemed to be glowing in that dim light between her red dress and thick black hair. She felt that the light appearing on Sita's face was not just the light of this dim lamp.

She was surprised and the thought 'Sita was indeed a goddess' came to her mind once again, then she looked at Ram. He was still sleeping.

Kausalya got up slowly, came out of the room and looked around the palace. Some lamps were still burning here and there. She came inside again, lay down with Ram's head close to her chest and tried to sleep.

11.
And Such a Morning

That morning also was like any other morning. Kaushalya began her day with a bath and proceeded to perform her puja. Once the puja was completed, she summoned Ram to her room. Upon his arrival, she asked him to call Kaikeyi.

Kaikeyi, somewhat taken aback by the early morning invitation, quickly made her way to the room. After she entered, Kaushalya instructed Ram to wait in the outer room for a while. Both Kaikeyi and Ram were left astonished by her request. Ram quietly rose and took his place in the outer room, awaiting further instructions. Kaushalya then took Kaikeyi's hand in her hand and said, "Kaikeyi, please be seated," guiding her to sit beside herself.

"Is there something important?" Kaikeyi inquired.

"Not particularly, but I have several matters to discuss with you today."

"Okay please," Kaikeyi replied.

"Kaikeyi, there was a time when I was very resentful towards you," Kaushalya confessed.

"I am aware of that but given my actions, it was just as expected. I hold no grievances against you or anyone else for that matter."

"However, that time has passed, Kaikeyi, and whatever has happened was probably destined for the dynasty of Ayodhya. Today, I have no ill will towards you."

This is your greatness and Didi (yelder sister), I am aware of your stature.''

"But Kaikeyi, I have not called you for this.''

"Then?'' Kaikeyi said.

"Kaikeyi, to date you have suffered so much of mental agony that hardly anyone else would have been able to bear, only due to a small mistake,.''

At this, Kaikeyi appeared sad and serious. Responding, she said "It was my fate."

"I feel sorrow for all the hurtful behaviour I may have exhibited during my moments of anger. Please forgive me, Kaikeyi."

"Didi, Why do you speak in such a manner?"

Kaushalya laughed at Kaikeyi's remark.

She said "Let us both extend forgiveness to each other," and before Kaikeyi could respond, she called for Ram.

"Ram."

"Yes," Ram replied as he approached.

"Where is Bharat?" Kaushalya inquired.

"I will check," Ram responded, leaving the room and returning with Bharat after a short while.

"Mother, did you call for me?" Bharat asked Kaushalya.

"Yes," she replied.

Bharat stood quietly before her.

"Bharat, may I pose a question to you?"

"Mother, if I am deemed worthy of it, then certainly."

"Bharat, if a truly good individual makes one mistake in life, is it just to subject him to suffering till eternity?"

The implications of Kaushalya's question were clear not only to Bharat but also to Kaikeyi and Ram. Given the recent events, Kaikeyi found the question not very surprising, while Ram and Bharat were taken aback.

Bharat hesitated before responding.

"Should we not consider the extent of the harm caused by that mistake?" Bharat suggested.

"Indeed, that is a valid point; however, often a significant loss is not attributable to a single cause but rather a series of factors," Kaushalya replied.

Bharat fell silent.

"You are not saying anything Bharat,"

"What should I say, I am not able to understand anything yet."

"Don't you believe that there had been a series of reasons behind the loss you are contemplating?"

Bharat remained quiet, but Ram interjected.

"Yes, there is indeed a lengthy chain of reasons involved."

"Bharat, this is your mother," Kaushalya indicated, gesturing towards Kaikeyi, "It is a grave error to overlook all the virtues of a person due to a single mistake in their life, Bharat."

And the after a brief pause, Kaushalya continued,

"Because of that one mistake, she has experienced both sorrow and shame, and I cannot imagine the extent of her mental anguish since that time. Bharat, you are doing a great injustice to her. Neither God nor nature, or the society grants us the right to inflict injustice upon anyone.

I too had a deep anger towards her. I had believed that her actions were the cause of your father's demise, yet I had overlooked the fact that she had once saved your father's life during the battle with Shambar and again during his severe illness.

These were significant events. Bharat, remember that curse given to the king by Shravan's blind parents, and then think, whether your mother Kaikeyi was not a mere instrument in this whole episode."

After making this statement, Kaushalya paused momentarily. Bharat remained silent, casting his gaze downward towards.

"I understand, Bharat, that there may still be lingering many questions in your mind," Kaushalya remarked.

In response, Bharat lifted his eyes to Kaushalya before lowering them once more.

"Bharat, you will recall that after Ram's exile to the forest, you attempted to persuade him to return to Ayodhya."

"Yes," Bharat affirmed.

"I was present with you during that time, as was your mother Kaikeyi."

"Indeed."

"And when we encountered Ram in Chitrakoot, are you aware that Kaikeyi also had a private meeting with Ram?"

Bharat did not respond. Kaushalya further said,

"You must know this, but do you also know how much Kaikeyi had cried, cursed her-self and apologized after seeing Ram and Sita?"

Bharat was unaware of this. He turned his eyes towards Ram.

"Mother is telling the truth, Bharat," Ram stated.

"And Bharat, for Ram and Sita, that episode of Kaikeyi ended that day. Have you ever seen their respect for Kaikeyi less than their respect for Sumitra or me?"

"No, but they are Ram and Sita. Not everyone can be Ram or Sita."

Bharat said.

"But you can try, right? And Bharat, also think that if Ram had not gone to Dandakaranya and Sita had not been kidnapped there, then the demon king Ravana would not have died at the hands of your brother and then how would the flag of the bravery of Ram, this Raghukul and Ayodhya be flying on this earth? Could the huge empire of Ayodhya be the same today?"

"What if Ravana had not died at the hands of my brother? But mother, because of that exile and kidnapping, my sister-in-law has suffered a lot of pain all her life. Our empire may have been small, but it would have been so good if she had not had to bear so much pain."

"Bharat, the respect you have for Sita and Ram is praiseworthy and the respect for them is not only in your mind but in the minds of so many people in this kingdom of Ayodhya and outside it and will remain for ages.

Bharat, do you think that Sita was so foolish that she would have mistaken a deer for gold? If she was really so fond of gold or such things, she would not have chosen to leave the palace and wander happily from forest to forest with her husband.

Exile was not given to her. And Bharat, don't you trust your brother's intelligence?

Do you think Ram would have believed that a live deer can be made of gold and not of flesh and bones and then he kept chasing that for a long distance and that dear kept running."

"No, neither Bhabhi (Sister-in-law Sita) had any kind of greed nor could brother believe the golden deer to be true.''

"Then don't you think that behind this, destiny was plotting the death of Ravana in this way.''

"Maybe.''

"And Bharat, you are the prince of Ayodhya, you have ruled Ayodhya for fourteen years and even today you have an active participation in the governance of Ayodhya. Has Ayodhya ever fought wars to expand its empire?"

"But it is the responsibility of the state to protect its borders, isn't it?"

"Yes but then the way Ravan was busy expanding his empire and had reached Dandakaranya in the south of Bharatvarsh, for how many more days could we have remained safe here in Ayodhya?"

"Not for many days."

"Then the war was fought on the enemy's land instead of our own, isn't that an achievement?"

"Yes."

"Won't you thank your mother Kaikeyi for this, Bharat?" Bharat was left speechless at this turn of Kaushalya's words, yet,

"Shall we leave aside the matter of the hardships faced by brother, sister-in-law and Lakshman in the forest?" he said.

"Bharat, the thought of the hardships faced by them in the forest troubles you a lot, doesn't it?"

"Yes."

"But think, if Raavan had reached here while expanding his empire, how much more powerful he would have become. Would defeating him at that time and then ousting him from Lanka also have been less painful than the sufferings endured in the forest?"

"No, but Bhabhi would not have had to suffer so much and go like this."

"How can you say this Bharat? Who knows who would have been sacrificed in what form in that terrible and big war, and sacrifices are a must in war, without this there is no war," said Kaushalya.

As she said this, she felt that perhaps there was some excitement in her voice and it had become a bit sharp, so she became quiet for some time, tried to calm her mind and said,

"Bharat, you are no less dear to me than Ram."

"I know very well, mother."

"Bharat, there is one more fact related to Ram's exile, which perhaps none of us has noticed."

"What?" Bharat said.

"Ram has spent fourteen years in the forest before becoming the king of an empire like Ayodhya. During that period, he himself walked and saw Bharvarsh from north to south. He met sages and saints as well as the people from the lowest and poorest section of the society very closely. He saw and understood their lives. This experience is not a small thing.

How many kings get the opportunity to connect with their public in this way. Perhaps this was his experience due to which he could establish such a rule in which the weaker section also has the same civil rights as the established and powerful section of the society and the difference between the rich and the poor has also reduced.

This Ram Rajya will remain the concept of an ideal state for the coming generations and the contribution of the fourteen years spent by him in the forests will be very big. So Bharat, shouldn't Kaikeyi also get the credit for this Ram Rajya?'' Kaushalya asked,

With this statement of Kaushalya, Bharat found himself back to where he was a while ago when he had agreed that Kaikeyi should be given the credit for the Ram-Ravan war not being fought on Ayodhya's land but on the enemy's land.

Everything Kaushalya said seemed true to him and his anger towards his mother Kaikeyi was also reducing, but still, perhaps, something was left somewhere. He did not answer Kaushalya's question this time as well.

Kaushalya was aware that the way she was supporting Kaikeyi for so long, Kaikeyi was feeling shy. She said to Bharat,

"Bharat, look at your mother. She is feeling shy with just a little praise of herself. What will you say about this humility?"

Ram was still listening quietly. With the intention of including him in this conversation, Kaushalya pointed towards him and said,

"Ram, during the churning of the ocean, both nectar and poison were produced. Everyone was eager to drink the nectar, but only Shiva came forward to drink the poison. Kaikeyi, who was the reason behind your creation of the Ram Katha, has taken all the evil and the infamy on herself.

Kaikeyi, who has drunk all the poison alone like Neelkanth Lord Shiva, is indeed worthy of respect.

We are not just a body. The five elements of which this body is made, earth, water, air, fire, and sky, are also only means. To reach the goal, we will have to be observers."

"But how will we be able to resist injustice by being only observers?"

"You are right Bharat, we should resist injustice with all our might, but being an observer is not a hindrance in that too. We should have a punishment in one hand but there should be simplicity and forgiveness in the other.

It is fine to remain unperturbed in happiness and sorrow, but the difference between right and wrong should be made not on the basis of beliefs but on the basis of the voice that arises from within."

"You are right, mother."

"So, could I make you understand my point Bharat?"

"I have completely understood your words and yes, I completely agree with them but I will be able to say this affirmately only after implementing them in my life."

"Then will you accept one request of mine?''

"Mother, I am committed to comply with any of your orders.''

"Not an order Bharat, orders are accepted by the mind, but requests are accepted by the heart.''

"Whatever you say, mother, I will accept it from the heart.''

"Your mother has the right to get respect and love from you, do not deprive her of this. Whatever anger you have in your heart against her, give up on it, Bharat,'' said Kaushalya. Bharat was expecting something similar from Kaushalya. The truth is that after Kaushalya's persuasion for so long, his anger towards Kaikeyi had ended and there seemed no point in holding on to an old matter, but the behaviour he had become accustomed with to towards Kaikeyi over the years was preventing him from reacting to Kaushalya's words.

Significant time had elapsed since this discussion. Sumitra had learned of Kaushalya's conversation with Kaikeyi, Bharat, and Ram. The length of their dialogue was somewhat surprising.

Sumitra had begun to sense that something significant was unfolding. Concerned, she stepped outside Kaushalya's room and called out, "Sister, may I enter?"

"Yes, come in, Sumitra; I was just about to summon you," Kaushalya replied.

Sumitra entered and took a seat beside her, inquiring, "Is everything alright? The sun has risen high in the sky, and you all have been here since morning. Not only I, but the daughters-in-law are also quite anxious."

Kaushalya chuckled, "It is nothing of the sort; I was simply enjoying the conversation."

Bharat remained silent. Kaushalya seized the opportunity once more, turning to Bharat and stating, "There is one more matter, Bharat. Based on my understanding of Sita, I can assert that if she were present today, she would have advised you that any feelings other than respect and love for your mother are inappropriate."

Pausing a little, Kaushalya said again, "Bharat, no one knows anything about life, but still Kaikeyi and I are in the last stages of our lives. Any of our breaths can be our last at any time."

"Mother, please express whatever you wish, but refrain from making such statements," Bharat implored.

"Bharat, I have conveyed all that I intended to say."

"Well," Bharat responded, bowing to Kaikeyi's feet.

"Mother, please forgive me," he said to Kaikeyi.

Kaikeyi embraced Bharat tightly, tears streaming down her face as she called out, "Son." The intensity of her emotions resonated within Bharat, causing his heart to race palpably in his chest. They both wept together, a touching reunion between a mother and her son who had been separated for years. The moment was beyond description.

Time seemed to freeze in that instant. Silence enveloped the room, and an unspoken turmoil stirred within everyone present. Gradually, Kaikeyi and Bharat regained their composure, while Ram and Sumitra appeared to emerge from a distant place.

"I have honoured my vow to him," Kaushalya stated before closing her eyes.

"What was that vow?" Ram inquired, but Kaushalya remained silent, her eyes still shut, lost in her thoughts.

"The respect and honour for Didi Kaikeyi will remain unchanged; it must have always been so," Sumitra remarked.

It was very late, but Kaushalya was still sitting motionless with her eyes closed, not reacting to anything. Everyone was waiting for her to open her eyes, but when she did not open her eyes for a long time and there was no movement in her body, Ram touched her shoulder with his hand, shook her gently and said 'Maan'.

With this, Kaushalya fell down while sitting. Everyone was stunned, she had gone for ever. Perhaps she had successfully completed the last task of her life and now she had no desire to see or hear anything else.

"No, you cannot do this, Didi. You cannot leave me alone and go like this. No, no, no...." Kaikeyi started crying loudly. Hearing her voice, the daughters-in-law and others also came.

Everyone was weeping except Ram. He was very shocked. 'What has happened?' he said to himself. Suddenly he felt some pain in his chest and his eyes filled with tears. A slight smile full of pain came on his lips. His lips were slightly tilted.

He shook his head slightly and keeping his hand on his chest, moved a little away to have the support of a wall of the room. There, he rested his head against the wall and closed his eyes.

He felt as if darkness had surrounded him and then after a while, he started seeing many images of Kaushalya's loving nature.

He felt as if her breathing had also slowed down.

The sounds of people coming and going, some painful talks, and some wailing voices were heard. He was still feeling pain in his chest. Don't know what was in his mind but Ram said a long 'no...' to himself, then opened his eyes and said to himself in a very low voice,

"Let there be one more pain,"

After this, he moved his fingers on his forehead and then on his face thus trying to become normal and went forward to console Kaikeyi.

One more sacrifice
One more pain
Seized the heart
Still this silence

12.
And Kaikeyi

Bharat's behaviour towards Kaikeyi had changed completely. He had started taking a lot of care of her. He probably wanted to make up for his behaviour towards Kaikeyi till now.

It had been a considerable period since Kaushalya's departure. Kaikeyi frequently sensed the absence of her husband, as well as that of her goddess-like daughter-in-law Sita and her elder sister-like Kaushalya. She had started feeling very lonely.

Following the departures of Dasharatha, Sita, and subsequently Kausalya, Kaikeyi had gradually become more introverted. Her silence had become increasingly pronounced.

This silence was a source of concern for those around her, particularly for, Bharat's wife Mandvi, who felt especially troubled by it. She brought her worries to Bharat. This silence of Kaikeyi was bothering her a lot.

The truth was that although Bharat's immense respect and loving behaviour had given Kaikeyi a lot of mental peace, Kaushalya's sudden departure had increased her mental agony a lot.

She would often go into a state of depression, so Mandavi and Bharat started trying to talk to her and spend more time with her.

Mandavi was very worried about Kaikeyi. One day when Kaikeyi was sitting alone thinking about something, Mandavi went to her and said,

"Mother, can I sit next to you?"

"Yes, Mandavi," Kaikeyi replied. Mandvi settled beside her and asked,

"Mother, why do you remain so quiet? Is something troubling you?"

"No, everything is well."

"Then why this profound silence?"

"But what is there to say?"

"I sense you remain preoccupied with thoughts."

"Indeed, I am. I often reflect on how sister Kaushalya departed like a yogi, without pain, without medicine, and without the need for anyone's service.

Even after death, there was no change in her face. It seems as if some divine power had gently guided her. Just as she lived her life peacefully, she decided to leave this world peacefully too. What a pious soul she must have been."

"Certainly."

"Mandavi, sometimes I think, what will happen to me?"

"Mother, why do you think such things?"

"Just like that, sometimes this thought comes to mind."

"No, don't think all this. What is the use of worrying about something that is not in our hands,"

"You are right, Mandavi," said Kaikeyi.

Mandavi sat for some more time. Talks about Kaushalya and Sita dominated the conversation. When the evening started to fall, Mandavi said,

"Mother, shall I go?"

"Yes daughter, you will be having some work."

After Mandvi departed, Kaikeyi remained seated for a short period before rising to go to her bedroom, where she sat on the bed and closed her eyes, attempting to meditate on the divine. She lost track of time until the voice of a maid broke her concentration.

"Queen Mother, it is night time; everyone is awaiting your presence in the dining room."

"I am not hungry, my daughter. Please inform everyone that I will not be dining at this hour," Kaikeyi responded. The maid felt a surge of joy at being addressed as 'daughter.'

"Mother, please go and have some thing atleast . It will not be good to sleep on an empty stomach," she said. Then she felt shy when she addressed Kaikeyi as 'mother' instead of 'queen mother', although this address had slipped out of her mouth inadvertently on hearing the word 'daughter' used for herself.

"No, my daughter, I truly have no appetite. Kindly convey my apologies to everyone."

The maid paused, contemplating Kaikeyi's words. She once again referred to herself as 'daughter' and sought forgiveness from the others for her absence at the meal. "What has come over the Queen Mother?" she wondered. Noticing the maid still standing, Kaikeyi said,

"Please go now, my daughter; I wish to meditate a while longer."

"Very well, Mother, I shall take my leave," the maid replied. After her departure, Kaikeyi resumed her meditation in the same manner.

The maid went to the dining room and told about Kaikeyi. It was okay that she did not wish to take anything, but no one could understand the idea of apologizing for this.

Bharat got up to go to her but Mandavi stopped him and told everyone about what had happened with Kaikeyi a while ago and then said,

"Looking at the state of her mind at that time, I think it would be better not to disturb her peace.''

On hearing this from Mandavi, Bharat sat back in his seat.

"You finish your meal, after that, I will go and see her.''

"I too, will accompany you," said Bharat.

"Okay.'' said Mandavi. Actually, she was thinking that if Bharat left his meal and got up, then seeing Kaikeyi's state of mind, she did not know whether he would come and sit for the meal again. When the meal was over, Bharat said to Mandavi,

"Let us go.'''

"Yes.'' said Mandavi.

When they reached Kaikeyi's room, she was sitting in a very calm posture with her eyes closed. Hearing the sound of their arrival, she opened her eyes. Seeing Bharat and Mandavi, she laughed softly.

"Come, sit," saying this she pointed towards the seat.

"Mother, why didn't you come to take food?" Bharat said.

"Nothing serious, I don't know why I don't feel like eating anything. Have you taken your dinner?"

"Yes," Bharat confirmed.

"And you, Mandvi?" Kaikeyi asked.

"I will eat later," Mandvi replied.

"No, you should go and eat first, then we can spend some time together," Kaikeyi insisted.

Mandvi rose and said, "Mother, you could have had something."

"I have no desire for food," Kaikeyi replied.

Mandavi stood up and said,

"Mother, you please have something atleast"

“No, I don’t want anything.”

“Okay, then just a little milk,” Mandavi said.

“No, nothing,” Kaikeyi said, but Bharat made a light gesture to Mandavi, which meant that she should go and get milk. Mandavi went brought some milk in a vessel.

“Mother, there is a little milk, please have it,” she said and Bharat also requested her.

“Though I don’t want it but I know, you people won’t agree,” Kaikeyi laughed, took the milk, and started drinking it slowly. Mandavi was standing. After finishing the milk, Kaikeyi kept the vessel on the ground and said to Mandavi,

“Sit down, why are you standing.”

Mandavi sat down where she was. Bharat was still standing. Kaikeyi said to Bharat and Mandavi,

“Not there, both of you please come nearer and sit beside me.”

When both of them came and sat near her, Kaikeyi held Bharat’s hand in one hand and Mandavi’s hand in the other and started looking at them.

“Do you want to say something mother?” Bharat said.

“Yes,”

“What?”

“I don’t know,” saying this Kaikeyi laughed.

They sat quietly like this for some time. The night was getting darker. Kaikeyi said,

“Bharat, Mandavi, it is getting dark, now both of you, go and sleep.”

“You go to your room and sleep there, but I will sleep here only,” Mandavi said to Bharat.

"No Mandavi, there is no need to worry, I am absolutely fine," said Kaikeyi and after much insistence sent Bharat and Mandavi to their room, after which Kaikeyi again sat quietly.

xxxxxxx

Kaikeyi remained in meditation for a long time and after it was late at night, she lay down on the bed. The things that happened with Mandavi in the evening were still going on in her mind, but Kaikeyi, exhausted physically and mentally, started feeling sleepy. In a short while, she started getting lost in her dreams.

And now probably, this too was a dream. She saw that Kaushalya, as if flying, came from the window of her room and stood in the air, some distance above the ground, from her bed. Kaikeyi felt that she was coming from somewhere very far. Kaikeyi was lying on the bed, she got up and sat, pointed towards the bed, and said,

"Didi, please come and sit."

Kaushalya came closer but did not sit. She remained still in the air.

"Have you come alone?" Kaikeyi asked.

"No, Sita is with me," Kaushalya responded.

"Where is she?"

"Here she is," Kaushalya pointed beside her.

Kaikeyi then noticed Sita standing there as well. She alternated her gaze between Sita and Kaushalya.

"Kaikeyi," Kaushalya called.

"Yes, Didi."

"Why do you remain sad and quiet so much? Is there still some shortcoming in Bharat's behaviour?"

"Didi, ever since you explained the things to him, his behaviour has changed completely. Now he gives me a lot of love and respect."

"Then."

"Earlier I used to talk a lot, I have seen its bad effects. Now I feel that it is better to remain quiet."

"And why do you remain sad?"

Kaikeyi laughed at this question and said

"Perhaps the mind has become used to being sad while enduring pain, and Didi, after your departure, this loneliness hurts a lot,''

"I know your mind, Kaikeyi, but don't worry; this will not always be the same.''

"I know Didi,'' Kaikeyi said and then said to Sita,

"Sita, you will not say anything. Are you still annoyed with me?''

"Mother, I have never been annoyed with you, not even when we had to go into exile; but I was just unable to think of what to say."

"Daughter, would you come closer? May I embrace you just once?"

"Yes, why not? It will be my good fortune." Sita said, approaching Kaikeyi and embracing her. After a while, when Kaikeyi released her, Sita stepped back and stood beside Kaushalya.

The moment was deeply emotional for Kaikeyi, who, while holding Sita, repeatedly murmured, "This my daughter," as she gently stroked Sita's back.

"Kaikeyi, shall we go?'' said Kaushalya.

"So soon.''

"Yes, I have to go, but I want to tell you one thing.''

"What?''

"Nobody has seen you laughing for a long time, and if I am not mistaken, then not at all since King Dasharath's death and then after Bharat returned from his maternal grandparent's house and refused to accept the throne of Ayodhya.''

"I do laugh, Didi but at my wit and my misfortune.''

"I am feeling hurt by your talks, Kaikeyi. If you were a little girl, I would have tickled you so much that you would have rolled on the floor laughing.''

On hearing Kaushalya say this, Kaikeyi laughed and so did Sita.

"Yes, this is the scene I longed to witness. You are truly lovely, and your laughter is even more enchanting. Being trapped in memories not only ruins the present but also obstructs the path to the future. If there is life, there is sorrow, Kaikeyi, but do not get attached to sorrow. Having said this, Kaushalya announced her departure and said, "I take my leave now." And having said so, she went out of the window, taking Sita with her, just as she had come.

'I wish I could also fly anywhere like this,' thought Kaikeyi. She kept watching Kaushalya and Sita leaving and then closed her eyes. She felt as if she was very tired of walking in this journey of life. She remembered the time when she was full of energy.

She remembered the days spent at her father Anaava's place in her maternal home Kekaya and then her war skills in the war between Maharaj Dashrath and Asurapati Shambar.

xxxxxxx

King Aanava of Kekaya was from the lineage of Janamejaya and

Kekaya was a prosperous and powerful kingdom. Kaikeyi was Aanav's daughter. The youngest, very beautiful and endowed with many qualities, Kaikeyi was her father's most beloved child. Aanava had also taught her horse-riding, chariot-driving and weapon-handling and he used to take her along with him to hunts and wars.

Among Dasharatha's wives, Kaushalya was the daughter of Koshal King Bhanumaan and Sumitra was the princess of Magadha.

Dasharatha had no children when he had asked for Kaikeyi's hand from Kekaya King Aaanav. When he asked for Kaikeyi's hand in marriage from the Kekaya king Aanav, Aanav put forth a condition to give the kingdom of Ayodhya only to the son of his beloved daughter, which Dasharath gladly accepted.

Later Dasharatha, impressed by Kaikeyi's war skills, used to take her along with him to wars. He also took Kaikeyi along, in the war with Asura Pati Shambar, the husband of the elder sister of Ravana's wife Mandodari. Thirty-six Asura kings like Prakampan, Vajrapanjar, Vikataksha had also come to support Shambar in this war, and apart from Panchal King Divodas, Dasharatha also had many other valiant kings on his side.

After the armies of both sides came face to face, the sound of conches and the beating of drums started. When the battle began, there was a fierce rain of arrows from both sides. Many demon kings had came forward to help Shambar, who was facing Dasharath's attacks, and started attacking him from all sides. Both Dashrath's bow and chariot broke in this attack. He started fighting on foot, with a sword only, but soon his body was riddled with wounds.

Kaikeyi was driving Dasharath's chariot. After the chariot broke, Kaikeyi came forward to protect him with a bow and arrow. The demon kings, wounded by the fierce rain of arrows by her, started leaving the battlefield, then Shambar himself came forward.

Kaikeyi had become a warrior goddess. Her face was turning red with anger and brilliance. Shambar was surprised to see this form of Kaikeyi.

"Brave lady, can I know your identity".

"What purpose would my identity serve you, Shambar? We are all destined for death in one form or another."

"I do not engage in combat with women. Whoever you may be, step aside."

"I commend your sentiment; brave men indeed honour women. However, at this moment, I am neither a man nor a woman, but your adversity."

At that moment, someone informed Shambar that she was Kaikeyi, the wife of Dasharatha and the daughter of King Aaanav of Kekaya. In response, Shambar remarked, "Queen, I see the truth of what I have heard about you. While many may envy your martial heroism, I urge you once again to clear my path. I have no desire to raise arms against any woman."

"Shambar, set aside notions of gender and engage in battle. I have come forth as your death."

Shambar laughed at it, which only served to provoke Kaikeyi further.

"Do not forget, Shambar, that Mother Durga, who vanquished Shumbh and Nishumbh, is also a woman," she asserted, and while defending Dasharatha, she unleashed to shower razor-sharp arrows once more.

Shambar defended himself by deflecting Kaikeyi's arrows with his own, deliberately refraining from shooting back at her. Kaikeyi recognized his restraint.

"Strike Shambar, or death will soon be upon you," Kaikeyi declared, exhibiting remarkable agility and valour in the battle.

"O Queen, death is certain and so is its time, I do not worry about it," Shambar said.

As the battle reached its climax, Maharaj Divodas, perceiving the peril faced by Dasharatha and Kaikeyi, advanced with firm resolve. Almost instinctively, he grasped Dasharatha's hand and pulled him into his chariot. Kaikeyi observed this development and swiftly approached them.

Divodas entrusted the reins of his chariot to Kaikeyi, leaping into another chariot to engage Shambar. Ultimately, it was Divodas in this fierce battle, who defeated Shambar.

Holding the reins of the horses with one hand and wielding the sword with the other, Kaikeyi displayed tremendous courage, skill, bravery and intelligence and took Dasharatha out of the battlefield.

After moving away from the battlefield, Kaikeyi took her chariot to a source of water. She took water from it, spoke some Mantras, thus enchanted the water, washed Dasharatha's face with the same water, gave him some water to drink, and then sprinkled the same water on his body. Dasharatha's unconsciousness started to reduce and so did the pain of the wounds. As soon as he regained some consciousness, Kaikeyi carefully brought him back to Ayodhya.

xxxxxxx

After remembering everything, Kaikeyi felt a surge of self-confidence and sat up. Thoughts were flowing inside her.

'What is left to be achieved now? There is nothing, and I don't have anything to leave behind' she thought. Then some thing came to her mind and she laughed softly.

Nothing is left to be achieved, nor anything is being left behind, still, I am here. So what if I am here and so what if I am not?' she said to herself.

Kaikeyi closed her eyes, sat with her head slightly raised and tried to experience infinity. It came to her mind that she was looking at a tree on which a bird was sitting and looking at a beautiful white flower blooming in the tree. 'If this flower was red, it would have looked even more beautiful', the bird thought and then looked around.

There were thorns on the tree too. 'I have to make the flower red', thinking this the bird placed its chest on a big thorn just above the flower and pressed it. The thorn pierced his chest and blood started flowing which started turning the flower red as it passed through the tree. The bird was looking at the flower. In a short while, the flower became completely red.'

'Yes, now it looks so good' it thought and rolled over with a terrible pain in her chest. Kaikeyi's body felt a thrill and her eyes opened. She took a deep breath and a light smile once again floated on her lips.

She folded her hands, closed her eyes and tried to immerse herself in the feeling of God.

'O God, you are the ultimate truth. You can neither be denied nor proven,' she thought.

You are such a concept beyond which nothing can be thought.

'I have wandered through so many jungles of thoughts, alone and helpless, to find you.

You are endowed with all qualities yet without any quality, capable of any change yet unchangeable, alone yet innumerable.

To find you is bliss, and the true effort to find you is also no small bliss.

And if this can happen anytime, anywhere and at any moment, then O God, make these moments of mine that one moment.

You are pure peace and never-ending bliss. Give me the feeling of being filled with this pure peace and bliss. Make me so alive and harmonious that I am filled with the feeling of your presence. Come, O God, come and hold my hands.'

Having said this, Kaikeyi stopped. 'God, I have nothing more to say,' she said to herself and she felt as if she was surrounded by a soft light and was filled with joy. She felt as if her forehead and palms had become more sensitive and she was feeling something that could not be described.

"God, you have come, right?" words came out from her lips and she laughed softly.

In a while, she started feeling as if she was filled with God's blessings and whatever was happening inside could only be felt.

She felt coolness, purity and seriousness spread all around her and also felt an untouchable softness and a strange sweet smell. She was feeling very good. Kaikeyi started to feel a little sleepy. She involuntarily rolled over and lay down on the bed.

It was a wonderful situation, full of bliss. She had never experienced such a thing before. She was overwhelmed. 'And what is this?' Kaikeyi felt as if she was floating in the air and could also see her own body lying below.

'Oh, I can fly,' she thought. 'Just like Kaushalya and Sita had come.' She was filled with wonder and then came out of the room floating in the air. She felt that the light she had felt in the room was still around her.

She came out and saw that it was not night. It was like dawn. She saw trees below, their shadows, and the sky above with a wonderful blueness. The sun was not visible.

She started rising upwards just by wishing. Unburdened, Kaikeyi reached very high, but that divine and gentle light was still with her. Slowly, the sense of belongingness started to fade and she started feeling as if she was nothing but a part of that light.

xxxxxxx

It was late in the morning. The people of the royal palace were busy in their respective works. But it was surprising that Kaikeyi, who used to wake up very early every day, had still not come out of her room. Bharat and Mandavi reached her room worriedly. Kaikeyi was still sleeping. Mandavi touched her feet, shook her and called out,

"Mother", but there was no answer.

Bharat touched her face and turned it towards him. Her head rolled down. She had left this world.

13.
Some Miscellaneous Too

Sumitra was the only one left among the elders of the family. She was the only one who used to call Ram as 'Ram'. She used to talk to him saying 'tum', showering her affection. Whenever Ram used to touch Sumitra's feet, he used to feel that so many people wanted to touch his feet and expect his blessings, but only these feet of Sumitra were the ones which he could touch to get blessings. Ram had started taking special care of her and tried to ensure that she did not feel lonely, but Sumitra could not live for long. She too followed the path of Kaushalya and Kaikeyi within a few days.

xxxxxxx

Kekaya, where Kaikeyi's maternal home was, Maharishi Gargya, son of sage Angira, had come as Kekaya's messenger. Today's Punjab was Kekaya at that time. Kaikeyi's father had passed away and her son Yudhajit was the king there. Maharishi Gargya had brought with him many horses, gems and jewellery as gifts.

When the news of his arrival reached Ayodhya, Ram along with his brothers went ahead to welcome him.

The Gandharvas ruled the region to the west of Punjab up to present-day Afghanistan. This region was called Gandharva Desh or Gandhar and probably that is why the residents here were called Gandharvas. They were mostly tall, fair and strong. Gandharvas were repeatedly attacking Yudhajit. Sage Gargya had come to Ayodhya on behalf of King Yudhajit with a request for help him against the Gandharvas.

Ram without delay sent Bharat with his two sons Taksha and Pushkal and a huge army to help Yudhajit. A fierce battle took place between King Yudhajit of Kekaya who had received Bharat's help and the Gandharvas. Yudhajit was killed in this battle, but the Gandharvas were badly defeated. Bharat divided the kingdom of the Gandharvas between his sons Taksha and Pushkal. Bharat stayed there for five years and strengthened their kingdoms and then returned to Ayodhya.

Two new cities named Takshashila in Taksha's kingdom and Pushkaravati in Pushkala's kingdom were established and made the capitals of these kingdoms. Pushkaravati is now known as Peshawar.

Shatrughna had already captured Madhupur by killing the demon Lavanasur on Ram's orders. After some time, he divided that kingdom too, into two parts between his sons Subahu and Shatrughati. Subahu became the king of Mathura and Shatrughati of Vidisha.

For Lakshman's sons, both Ram and Lakshman wished that a beautiful and healthy place should be selected which was not in the territory of any other king, so that none's kingdom is snatched away, no war takes place, no blood is shed, no ashram or house is destroyed. For this, everyone liked the Himachal Pradesh situated in the lap of the Himalayas.

In this region, suitable Seetes were chosen, leading to the establishment of cities named Angadiya for Angad and Chandrakanta for Chandraketu. Both locations were noted for their beauty and safety. Prince Chandraketu, known for his immense strength, contributed to his kingdom being referred to as 'Malla Desh.'

Sometimes it occurred to Ram that his work was over. His mother, father and wife were all gone. His sons were grown up and capable. The kingdom of Ayodhya was strong and well established and there was peace and happiness in the kingdom. He had lived the Brahmacharya and Grihastha Ashrams, now it was time for Vanaprastha. He felt that Saryu had a special significance in his life. He had grown up drinking the water of Saryu, eating the food from the fields irrigated by it and playing on its banks.

Sometimes he used to remember that once while talking on the banks of Saryu he had said to Sita that Saryu was like a mother to him.

Even today he felt that even in Vanaprastha he would not want to go far from Saryu and would like to spend the rest of his life in some peaceful place on it's banks. The sons of his brothers had automatically established themselves in different kingdoms. For his sons and for the kingdom of Ayodhya, he had a feeling that someday he would sit with all three brothers and decide in this regard.

14.
Colours of Time

An ascetic had arrived as a messenger of Maharishi Atibal, seeking an audience with Ram. Lakshman encountered him outside Ram's palace.

"O sage, how come you came here?" Lakshman inquired.

"I have come as an envoy of Maharishi Atibal, with a message for Shri Ram," the ascetic responded.

"Very well, please wait a moment while I inform him about your arrival," Lakshman replied before entering the palace to seek Ram's approval and the ascetic was then invited inside. Ram rose to greet him and offered him a seat.

"I am the messenger of Maharishi Atibal with a message," the ascetic stated.

"I am honuored that Maharishi Atibal has remembered me. Please convey his message," Ram requested.

Instead of responding, the ascetic began to observe the surroundings.

"His message is confidential and intended solely for you," he said.

"There is no one else present except for us," Ram replied.

"However, someone might interrupt our discussion."

"Very well, I will instruct Lakshman to ensure that no one enters without my consent."

"Please wait, Maharaj. Maharishi Atibal has declared that if anyone interrupts our conversation, he will face the death penalty from you. I will disclose the message only when I receive this assurance from you."

Ram was taken aback by the ascetic's revelation regarding the challenging condition. He envisaged the nature of the message that Maharishi could convey. His thoughts wandered; if someone tried to approach despite Lakshman's intervention, that individual would not be an ordinary person, and it raised the question of whether he would be deserving of death penalty by him.

"It appears that Maharaj is deep in contemplation," remarked the ascetic.

"The person who disobeys Lakshman will not be an ordinary person. He may even be invincible for me. If it was not in my upbringing to not disobey the sages, I would have outrightly rejected this condition," Ram said.

"Think, if there is a sage and he becomes adamant, can we kill him?" Ram added. It was as if he was looking into the future.

"You are right, but Maharishi Atibal wants this."

"I want you to put my doubts before him and ask him to reconsider his condition once again.

"Very well, I shall return after discussing your message with him. I must take my leave now," the ascetic said.

"However, please stay for a moment; allow us the opportunity to extend our hospitality," Ram urged.

"Do not concern yourself with that, Maharaj. I am entirely content with your delings, and had I not been pressed to deliver this message to you as early as possible, I would have stayed a while longer," the ascetic replied before taking his leave.

The ascetic left but left a big question in Ram's mind. He could not forget the thought of 'what the message would be'. His mind became somewhat apprehensive. 'Surely something special is going to happen,' Ram thought. The ascetic appeared again the very next day.

' Please come, be seated', saying this Ram welcomed him.

'Maharaj, I had told Maharshi about your apprehension,' he said as he took his seat.

'Then?'

'He has said that he can understand that a person who disobeys Lakshman and enters your palace can also be a very important person or a sage.'

'Then?' Ram asked.

"The sage has said that in that situation the person on guard will be subjected to the harshest punishment by you and I can give you this message only after taking this promise from you."

'What kind of message will this be, Ram thought, but it was not possible for him to disregard the sage.

"Okay," he said, called Lakshman and said,

"Laxman, tell whoever is at the gate that as long as this ascetic is with me, no one should come inside otherwise he will be subjected to the harshest punishment by me."

Lakshman felt that there must be something special otherwise Ram would not have given such an order. If the person coming is a special person then he can also disobey the gatekeeper. In such a situation, not only will the conversation between Ram and the ascetic be interrupted, but the innocent gatekeeper will get a very harsh punishment. 'I myself will take up this task of Ram' he thought and after sending the gatekeeper away, he himself stood there as a gatekeeper.

After getting alone in the room, Ram said to the ascetic,

"Mahatma, now you can say without hesitation whatever you want to say."

"Then, I am repeating the message of Maharishi Atibal for you in his own words."

"Okay, tell me," Ram said.

"Maharaj, he has said that Lord, the work for which you had come is now complete."

Ram was a little surprised when he heard this message. Maharishi was saying the same thing which he himself had been thinking for the last few days. What an amazing coincidence, he thought. He was also surprised when Maharishi addressed him as 'Prabhu'. He had often heard that 'He is not an ordinary human being. He is an incarnate person."

Today, with this message from Maharshi, he felt that probebly he is not an ordinary person but something different, something special and with this thought, a smile spread on Ram's lips.

Seeing Ram smiling like this, the ascetic was surprised and started looking at Ram's face.

"What else did Maharshi say?" Ram asked.

"He said that he is just reminding you. You have to take the decision."

"Okay," Ram said.

"Lord, what are your orders for me?" the ascetic asked.

Before Ram could say anything, he heard some noise at the door. In fact, Maharshi Durvasa had come. He wanted to meet Ram immediately and was not ready to listen to anything.

When Laxman stopped him, he became so angry that he started talking about cursing the entire family of Ram and then Laxman decided that it was better that he alone should bear the punishment of Ram rather than the entire family becoming the victim of Durvasa's anger. He became silent. Maharishi Durvasa pushed him aside and went inside.

Ram was startled to see him. Perhaps he has some urgent work with me,' he thought and said while greeting,

'Come Maharishi, are you alright?'

'Ram, I am very hungry.'

'All right Maharishi,' Ram said but he found it very strange. He could have told Laxman about his hunger outside and Maharishi would have been given the best food as per his wish.

This behaviour of Durvasa bothered him a bit, but he did not say anything. When he finished eating, Ram said,

"Maharishi, please take some rest."

"No", he said and left after giving his blessings. Ram was surprised at this behaviour od Durvasa.

Durvasa's arrival had interrupted the conversation between Ram and the ascetic. The ascetic asked again,

"Prabhu, what are your orders for me?"

"Please tell Maharishi that I have understood his words."

"And what about Durvasa's arrival?" the ascetic asked.

"Durvasa had come after you had conveyed Maharishi's message, so it is certain that he would not have heard it."

"Still his entry was before our talks were complete."

–"Okay I have got the message and whoever is guarding the door will receive the harshest punishment from me."

"Okay, Prabhu, please allow me to take your leave." the ascetic said.

"Pranaam" Ram said and the ascetic took his leave. After the ascetic left, Ram called Lakshman. Lakshman came.

"Who was at the door?" Ram asked.

"I Myself," Lakshman replied.

Upon hearing Lakshman's response, Ram fell into deep contemplation. He had sensed Lakshman's voice amidst the uproar when Durvasa arrived but had not considered that the gatekeeper would be absent and that Lakshman himself would be on duty. Lakshman, who had always been his faithful support, would have to bear the harshest consequences for no fault on his part.

Ram's heart trembled. He felt that the time had really come to fulfill the message hidden in Maharishi Atibal's message. All his work was over. He would have to return, but what punishment should he give to Lakshman.

He felt that Durvasa's arrival on this occasion and that too in this manner must also be a part of some special task, controlled by destiny.

'Perhaps this is a way to break his last attachment to the world, which is naturally with Lakshman', Ram thought. He was also thinking in his mind that what if he did not fulfill his promise of punishing Lakshman?

His fame will be tarnished, but whether his fame more valuable than Lakshman?

xxxxxxx

Ram was surrounded by many questions and doubts. Lakshman knew that he was liable to be punished and he felt that Ram would soon give him some harsh punishment, but his silence for so long had started disturbing Lakshman.

He had understood that Ram would be feeling pain at the very thought of punishing him and was perhaps in some confusion. This pain should not deter him from his words, Lakshman thought. He decided something in his mind, came to Ram and said,

"Brother."

"Yes," saying this Ram woke up as if has startled from sleep.

"I have made a mistake and am liable to be punished. Why are you hesitant in fulfilling your words? This is not in accordance with the dignity of Raghukul and your reputation."

"My reputation is not that great Lakshman."

"How great is your reputation, who knows it better than me?"

Ram did not answer Lakshman to this, only softly said "hmm" and walked away.

"Brother," Lakshman called out from behind.

"Yes Lakshman?" Ram said.

"Are you worried because your punishment will cause me pain?"

"Lakshman, any punishment I give you will cause me more pain than it will cause you."

Lakshman understood this truth, and upon hearing Ram's words, he felt a swell of pride in his fortune. "How deeply he loves me," he mused.

"Allow me to think over it, Lakshman," Ram stated as he departed, leaving Lakshman.

xxxxxxx

Ram was seated with sage Vashishtha, who also served as their family priest. He told the entire account of his dialogue with the ascetic sent by Maharishi Atibal, including his vow to punish the guard. Rishi Vashishtha too had the idea that all the tasks for Ram's arrival have been completed and the time for his departure must be near. Hence, he did not feel anything special upon hearing Maharishi Atibal's words. Yes, he did feel that death itself had come in the form of an ascetic.

But the thought of punishment for Lakshman at the hands of Ram disturbed him too. The Rishi knew that any pain to Lakshman would cause more pain to Ram, and here it was a matter of the harshest punishment.

This is such a harsh prelude to tomorrow, thought the Rishi. He was unable to decide what to say. The Rishi's silence increased Ram's restlessness.

"Why are you silent, Rishivar," said Ram.

"I was thinking about the implication of Maharishi Atibal's words."

"And what is that, Rishivar?"

"Ram, a person like you does not need me to explain the meaning of anything to me."

"Then."

"I am thinking about Laxman's punishment."

"Yes, get me out of this difficult situation, Rishivar."

"Ram, you have talked about the harshest punishment and the harshest punishment for any human being is death penalty."

On hearing Maharshi's words, Ram's heart beat very hard and the colour of his face changed.

"Death penalty for Laxman," he said to himself. With this, his breath stopped in his chest, his eyes closed his eyes for a moment and then his gaze fixed on the roof of the palace in search of some sky.

Maharshi saw this and called out, "Ram."

Ram looked up at him and pressed his lips together. His right hand instinctively formed a loose fist, and he exhaled with a sound of resignation. Maharshi noticed that Ram's face had become completely emotionless.

"Yes, Maharshi," he replied.

"However, receiving a death sentence from you would not be the most severe punishment for Lakshman."

"Why do you say so, Rishiwer?" Ram asked, wondering if any punishment could be worse than this.

"Because Lakshman respects and loves you so much that giving up his life for you or at your command would not be a punishment for him. Instead he may consider it as a blessing."

"Then," Ram continued.

"His separation from you will torment him more than a death sentence."

"Oh," Ram heaved a sigh of relief as he said this. He felt that abandoning Lakshman would be a great punishment for him as well, but perhaps he had to do this. The pain of separation from Lakshman was visible on his face.

The sage saw this, understood Ram's pain and also his compulsion to give proper advice.

"Any other solution?" Ram asked.

"I don't think so," saying this, Sage Vashishtha took leave from Ram.

Ram came out to see him off. He always used to greet him, but today he touched his feet, stopped for a while and when the sage raised his hand to bless him, Ram held his hand and placed it on his head.

"What has happened?" Maharishi asked.

"Nothing."

"I can understand your pain Ram, be patient and yes my blessings are always with you."

Ram did not say anything, just held his hand for some more time. Once again he bowed down and touched his feet again, then stood there in a deep thoughtful posture and kept watching the sage go away and after some time he returned to the palace walking slowly with very heavy steps.

xxxxxxx

When Ram came to the palace, seeing his very serious posture, no one dared to ask him anything. How much more will the void in life become after Lakshman also leaves? Where will Lakshman go after I abandon him? What will happen to Urmila? Will Lakshman take her also with him? Will Lakshman leave this kingdom and go to some forest or will he go to some kingdom other than Ayodhya? Will he give up his life?

Questions after question were arising in Ram's mind. Worries about Urmila's future were also troubling him. He felt that it would be good if Lakshman also took Urmila with him, otherwise, Urmila would not be able to live here alone.

A series of doubts and questions kept going on in his mind, but thinking that 'duty has to be fulfilled', he called Lakshman.

Lakshman came and stood in front of him. Ram called him, made him sit very close to him and took his hand in his hands.

Lakshman, I had never imagined even in my dreams that I would have to punish you," he said.

"What is wrong in punishing someone for his mistake? Rajdharma is above relationships. You should tell me my punishment without hesitation and I believe from my heart that it will not be bad. Moreover, not one but hundreds of Lakshmans can be sacrificed to protect the dignity of Raghukul and your prestige."

Ram heard Lakshman but did not say anything. He kept looking at the earth silently.

"Speak out brother, why are you so silent?" Lakshman said.

"Laxman, I will have to abandon you," Ram said.

"What?" Lakshman had not expected this at all. On hearing this, he felt as if lightning had struck him.

"Yes, Lakshman, I abandon you and this is your punishment."

"Why don't you give me the death penalty?"

"Death will separate everyone one day. We have no control over it. That is a compulsion, but being separated while alive is a bigger punishment for some people and we are among those very few people, Lakshman."

"Yes, being separated from you will be definitely the biggest punishment for me."

"Unfortunately I have already promised to give you the harshest punishment," saying this Ram started waiting for Lakshman's reaction. The pain inside was visible on Lakshman's face, it seemed as if he was unable to say anything even though he wanted to.

"Don't go by the bodies, Lakshman. We are not just this body and the difference in perspective brings a difference in our feelings of happiness and sorrow. Your mind is very pure. Lakshman, why don't you try to experience liberation, not the pain of losing something.''

"How can I consider separation from you as liberation?''

"If you think a little beyond the bodies, you will understand what I am saying. I myself am also trying to do the same.''

"Did you succeed?'' Lakshman asked.

Ram did not answer this question, he just looked at Lakshman with his lips pressed. Lakshman read Ram's eyes, saw the expression on his face and said,

"I have understood.''

After this, there was silence for some time, then Lakshman got up and bent down to touch Ram's feet. 'I will not get these feet again' came to his mind and then he placed his head at Ram's feet.

"Bless me for the last time,'' he said.

"My blesings are always with you," Ram said and embraced Lakshman, and they remained in that position for a while, seemingly reluctant to part. When they finally separated, Lakshman turned and exited the room with slow and heavy steps.

Ram continued to watch him leave. The impact of the previous events had forced both of them to exercise a great deal of restraint, yet their eyes were red and filled with tears.

I am Ram,
Pains still linger
And make eyes wet
How much agony
Can one endure
By clenching his lips

15.
Towards Departure

Lakshman came out of the palace and stood there. It seemed from his face that he was in deep thought. Perhaps he was thinking about which way to go.

He remembered Urmila. What would happen to her came to his mind and then he involuntarily started walking towards his residence to meet her. He was unable to think what he would say to Urmila there and how he would make her understand.

Lakshman knew that Urmila would insist on coming with him and would not agree to live without him under any circumstances. While walking, he paused once again.

He had not decided anything for himself yet. He remembered everything that Ram had explained to him, but still living without Ram appeared a meaningless living to him.

From childhood till today, he had never been separated from Ram. He had always felt that this body is only to serve Ram. Ram was not only his elder brother, but also his ideal and idol.

Lakshman remembered that Ram had said that we are not just bodies. He had talked about trying to experience liberation. Lakshman felt that it would be difficult for him to experience any kind of liberation in being away from Ram.

This was not possible for him, but if liberation from the body is thought of, he was confused. The question of Urmila arose in his mind again. Lakshman remembered that when he was going to the forest with Ram and Sita for fourteen years, then at least there was a hope for Urmila that he would return, but as of now, he was unable to give even that much assurance.

It was not difficult to imagine how Urmila must have spent those fourteen years. Definitly she would have suffered a lot of pain, but there must have been a consolation too, but today will she be able to understand that I cannot live away from my brother, so I am leaving her alone to suffer. Lakshman felt that he was committing a crime against Urmila.

Not being able to live without Ram was his own problem, but Urmila was being forced to pay the price for the same, again and again.

He was also unable to decide whether he should go to Urmila for a final farewell or not. What would he say to Urmila when he will be before her? He knew that he would not be able to say, 'I am going to give up my life, because it will be an unbearable message for Urmila.'

It was becoming difficult for Lakshman to come to a decision and increasingly challenging to determine the appropriate course of action. He resolved to visit Urmila without disclosing his impending departure and trying to remain normal. Although this would also be a deceit, but going without meeting her would be a grave injustice to Urmila.

With a heavy heart, Lakshman reached Urmila, although he was trying his best to look normal, but the signs of the inner struggle were visible on his face somewhere.

"Are you worried about something?" Urmila's first question itself troubled Lakshman. He laughed in an attempt to look normal,

"No," he said. Urmila felt that her laughter was also fake, she looked at Lakshman and said,

"But…"

"But what?"

"Why do I feel that you are worried about something, otherwise this is not the time for you to return home."

Lakshman laughed again.

"I was going somewhere and I felt a little thirsty. The house was nearby so I decided to come home and take some water."

Urmila found this statement of Lakshman very strange. He had never left his work and come home just to drink water, yet she got up and said,

"I will bring it right away."

From Urmila's expression and words, Lakshman realized that she was struggling to comprehend his statements and was feeling uneasy.

"You worry about me a lot, that's why you must be feeling uneasy. Actually your remembrance was also one of the reasons for coming here at this time." he said.

Urmila felt that Lakshman's words and behaviour were different from his usual. She curled her lips, shook her head as if she did not understand anything and went to get water. When she returned, she had some eatables too, but Lakshman took only water.

"Please have something at least," Urmila requested.

"Oh, yes…" saying this Lakshman picked up a small piece of sweet and put it in his mouth, then held Urmila's hand and said,

"Urmila, you take so much care of me."

"Hmm?" Urmila looked at Lakshman, narrowing her eyebrows.

"And I am not able to give you enough time."

"Well, then please do so in future," Urmila said, looking at him.

"Urmila, if I had the ability to compose a song, it would be a magnificent melody filled with your emotions."

"Really!"

"It is said that there is a relationship between beauty and virtue."

"Is it so?"

"You, Urmila, embody that connection. You are the epitome of inner and outer beauty along with virtues."

"Hmm……..are you okay?" Urmila said and looked at Lakshman's face.

"Yes, why, what has happened to me?"

"I cannot tell you this, but something is definitely wrong.

"No, there is nothing."

"Don't tell if you don't want to, but there is something."

Lakshman understood that Urmila was not finding his behaviour normal.

"No, there is nothing," he countered and added,

"Okay, but now I want to go?"

Urmila was worried, she said,

"Please wait a little before you go."

Lakshman stopped. He remembered that Ram had said, 'Don't go only on the body, Lakshman. We are not only bodies.'

He looked at Urmila, a very beautiful female body was in front of him. He took his eyes off her, bowed his head, and looked at her again. Then, the words Ram had spoken came out of his mouth spontaneously.

"Don't go only on the bodies Urmila. We are not only bodies." Urmila was surprised by his sudden statement.

"That is?" she asked.

It seemed as if detachment had awakened inside Lakshman. He said,

"Look beyond the bodies also."

"How much?" Urmila was surprised by Lakshman's words.

"Beyond the body is the mind and beyond the mind is the soul. My body may be anywhere, but my mind is always with you.''

"I know, but what do you mean by talking about the soul?''

"The body is mortal, isn't it? But our souls are one, Urmila.''

"Why are you saying such things?'' Urmila said and to reduce the seriousness of the atmosphere, she came forward smiling and holding Lakshman's hand and said,

"I don't get into these big things. You are mine, and this is the biggest knowledge for me, but why are you saying such things today?''

"Nothing, just like that'' Lakshman said, tried to laugh, turned back, and went away.

His steps were heavy and not normal. Urmila kept watching him go. Lakshman's laughter also did not seem natural to her. She sat down worried. 'There is something' she said to herself and with fear in her mind she started remembering God.

xxxxxxx

Lakshman came out and started walking towards the Saryu and on reaching the bank he started walking along the bank of the Saryu in a state of uncertainty. So many thoughts and scenes were coming to his mind.

Even though he did not want to, he kept thinking about Durvasa. Always angry and ready to curse. Should such people be called sages?

Who can guess how many things and scenes were coming to his mind? Ram was always at the center of his thoughts and even today the moments spent with him were flashing in his mind repeatedly. He had always felt that he loved Ram the most, and to serve him was the goal of his life.

It was Ram's trust in him that he always chose him for difficult tasks. One such very difficult and unpleasant task was to leave Sita at Valmiki Ashram. He remembered that when Ram had asked him to do this most unpleasant task, he had very politely asked that if possible, it may please be done by someone else and not by him.

To this Ram had replied with a painful smile, 'If I do not ask you to do this then who else can be that trust worthy? Whom should I ask for this job, Lakshman?' And now when that very unpleasent message from Saint Atibal had come, he had trusted me to guard at the door.

Everyone has to go sooner or later, Lakshman thought. He had been following his elder brother all his life, but today when it was a turn to leave this world, he was going to surpass him. And as soon as this thought came to his mind, a slight smile came and curved his lips.

While walking, he closed his eyes and started meditating remembering the feet of Ram. Next, he imagined the lotus feet of Sita, whom he had been looking at, during the exile, bowed to them mentally and then opened his eyes. He found that while walking with eyes closed he had inadvertently come near the river. Lakshman stopped. He had come quite far from Ayodhya. Trees and fields were visible on both sides of the river. He saw a broken tree lying in the water near the river bank. Perhaps a storm had brought it down.

"The storm can bring down mighty trees; what am I in that comparison?" he thought laughing softly. Then he steadied himself against a tree that had fallen somewhat in the river.

xxxxxxx

Lakshman's thoughts turned to his mother, Sumitra, whose humility and simplicity were remarkable. She had always held Kaushalya and Kaikeyi in high regard, treating them as elder sisters, never seeking to assert her own significance.

She never discussed any of her sorrows, never complained, never showed any discontent. She always behaved naturally and simply.

Lakshman remembered that when he was going to the forest with Ram, she had not only gladly permitted him but also instructed him to always take care of his brother and sister-in-law and never let his service to them fall short. Furthermore, she had consoled Kaushalya, who was grieving Ram's absence, providing her with comfort and understanding.

As thoughts of the forest surfaced, he was reminded of Suparnakha—swift, unruly and defiant. It was her own mistake that her nose and ears were hurt, but how Suparnakha, feeling embarrassed and insulted, had made a story that I had cut off her nose and ears.

No one even thought that how it can be possible to cut someone's nose and ears with a sword.

Would not the individual in such a dire circumstance resist vehemently, resulting in numerous cuts and injuries to his face and hands?

There were no such injuries on Surpanakha's hands or face. Did she stand quietly and get her nose and ears cut?

Lakshman found himself laughing at the recollection of this event, pondering that had it not occurred, the subsequent kidnapping of his sister-in-law Sita and the eventual demise of Ravan might never have transpired.

Lakshman remembered the use of power by Meghnad in the war, his falling unconscious and Hanuman bringing the medicine. He also felt that had Hanuman not brought the medicine, he would have been fortunate to attain martyrdom and end his life at the feet of Shri Ram.

His thoughts then turned to his elder sister Shanta and her husband Shrang, and once again to Urmila. She would surely be waiting for him which will be a never-ending wait.

He envisioned Urmila anxiously awaiting his return till late at night, then sending his servants to look for him. In the meantime she will keep walking restlessly here and there, then she will sit down tired. Her eyes and head will be heavy and then when no attendant would have returned by nightfall, her sorrow would have manifested in tears, with the following day bringing the devastating news of his passing.

Lakshman shuddered at the thought of Urmila crying in pain. 'Urmila, you are very good. I am going to cause you pain once again, please forgive me,' he said to himself, then he felt that Urmila's more remembrance might weaken him.

He shook his head, as if he wanted to divert his attention from Urmila. He looked at the tree against which he was standing, stroked its rough bark, looked at the sky and then looked at the flowing river. After going some distance, the river appeared to be swirling a little and touching the clouds.

As Lakshman observed the river and its interaction with the clouds, he sensed Urmila's presence, envisioning her standing there, weeping and wiping away her tears. A shiver ran through him once more, prompting him to close his eyes.

My love
Despite a very long separation
We have lived togetherness
Do not perceive
This departing too
As a permanent severance
Beyond the clouds,
We shall unite again

He started trying to immerse himself in the meditation of God. 'The life of the body is due to the rhythm of heartbeats and this rhythm is bound to break.

Though Shivatva i.e. attaning qualities, powers and nature like Lord Shiv is beyond attainment yet, O God, I belong to You. I shall not perish; I will simply fade away.'

This thought crossed his mind. Gradually, his meditation deepened, and his breathing slowed. The stillness persisted for a while, with each breath becoming slower until it ceased altogether. And his motionless body set down in the river.

xxxxxxx

The news of Lakshman's departure was no less than a bolt of thunder for Urmila. It was clear to Urmila that he had come to meet her for the last time. After knowing the reason behind his departure, she was filled with anger towards Durvasa.

'Durvasa, your inappropriate actions have forced my noble and courageous husband to abandon his life in this manner. You have cast a shadow over my existence, inflicted immense suffering upon my esteemed brother-in-law Ram, and plunged all of Ayodhya into despair.

Now I, Urmila, wife of Lakshman, beseech the Divine that you may not meet an early demise. May you wander this earth for a long time, harbouring your anger, frightening others with your curses, and gathering their sighs,' Urmila silently prayed with her hands folded in devotion as she meditated on God.

It seemed as if Urmila had lost her senses after receiving the news of Lakshman's departure. As if she was walking on impulse, she reached in front of Ram's room.

There after receiving the news of Lakshman's departure, Ram had sent everyone out and closed the doors of the room. No one was allowed to come inside.

Urmila stood motionless in front of the closed door, her eyes fixed on it as if she were under hypnosis. After a while, she regained consciousness and muttered to her-self in a state of shock, 'How have I come here?' Then she turned to leave.

Ram was overwhelmed with tears inside his room, deep in countless memories of Lakshman. He had no desire to meet anyone. Suddenly, he sensed a presence at the door, as if someone were there to confront him with accusations. This made him restless, he glanced towards the door, but he found no one there; it was firmly closed. Rising from his seat, he walked to the door, opened it, and stepped out.

Urmila was in front of him, going back.

"Oh", the word came out of Ram's mouth and he got the reason for his uneasiness. Ram kept watching Urmila go silently and when she was out of his sight, he turned slowly with a heavy heart, came back to the room, went near a wall, clenched both his fists, pressed his lips, and banged the fists on the wall.

"Urmila, what should one do who cannot even cry?" Saying this he rested his head on the wall for a moment and then moved away.

Fighting the miseries
He kept walking
On the path of thorns
But yes
The pain overflowed
In the form of tears

xxxxxxx

Urmila returned from there and came to her room. Mandavi and Shrutkirti were there. On seeing Urmila, they came to her. Mandavi looked at her face. Urmila's face was as if she was staring somewhere into the void.

"Urmila", Mandavi called but there was no response.

"Didi", Shrutkirti said taking her hand in hers. Now Urmila said softly,

"Yes".

Despite Mandavi's efforts to make her sit in a proper place, Urmila sat down on the floor, put her head in Mandavi's lap, and started weeping. After a while, she raised her head and looking at Mandavi asked,

"Sister, why is fate so cruel?"

"I cannot say, Urmila," Mandvi replied, tears streaming down her face.

16.
The Last Leg

Lakshman's departure had sent a wave of grief through Ayodhya. Food was not cooked in many houses that day. Durvasa was the target of all. People were cursing him to death, but one question that was in everyone's mind was that since this was the second big blow for Ram after Sita's departure and would he be able to bear it? And in answer to this, everyone was unanimous on one point that it would not be easy for him to bear it.

Chitra was at home when Manas came back from somewhere. He was sad and depressed.

"Why are you like this?" Chitra asked.

"A disaster, a great disaster has happened."

Chitra was shocked to hear the words of disaster.

"What happened? Please tell me."

"Lakshman is no more."

"What are you saying?" Chitra asked, "But how did this happen?

Manas told whatever he had heard. Hearing this, Chitra sat on the ground with her hand on her forehead and started weeping.

"Chitra, what do you think will happen now?" Manas asked.

"A great misfortune has befallen us; Ayodhya will never be the same again."

"But why so? Our king Ram is there."

"He is there, but he will not be able to bear this blow."

"Yes, people outside also believed that it will be very difficult for him to bear this blow."

"It is not merely difficult; it will be utterly impossible for him to cope with this blow."

"What do you want to say, Chitra," Manas said.

"I don't know why I feel that he would like to leave the kingdom and go far away from here. He will not stay here."

"But who would agree to take responsibility of the kingdom in that situation?"

"Who knows, but it will not be good for Ayodhya," saying this Chitra stood up. She went and sat at the place of worship and started praying to God to save Ayodhya from any misfortune.

xxxxxxx

Chitra's words turned out to be true. Lakshman's death and Urmila's grief had disturbed Ram. While he had promised the messenger of Maharishi Atibal, he had not have anticipated such dire consequences, and the guilt of failing to foresee the potential outcomes weighed heavily on him.

He resolved to relinquish the kingdom to Bharat and withdraw from the world. Before making any final decisions, Ram contemplated discussing the matter with Bharat, Shatrughan, Rishi Vashishtha, and all the ministers to seek their approval, and thus he summoned them all.

Upon receiving the invitation, Bharat and Shatrughan were taken aback and felt a sense of unease. They had some indication of Ram's state of mind and wondered what he might reveal during this Council of Ministers meeting. Both Bharat and Shatrughan were left with questions.

As the meeting commenced, Ram addressed the allocation of kingdoms for Kush and Luv. After some deliberation, it was decided that Kush would be granted the kingdom of South Koshal, while Lav would receive the kingdom of North Koshal.

Following the determination of the kingdoms for Kush and Luv, Ram expressed, "I wish for Bharat to assume the throne of Ayodhya after my departure."

The proposal put forth by Ram took everyone by surprise. It was widely understood that Bharat, due to his deep affection for Ram, would reject this suggestion, and as Ram's eldest son, Kush was the rightful heir to the throne of Ayodhya. Bharat himself was greatly unsettled by Ram's proposal.

"Even the thought of life without you is a dreadful nightmare for me," he expressed.

"Bharat, do not allow sentimentality to cloud your judgment. The realm of Ayodhya has expanded significantly, encompassing eleven other kingdoms. It is imperative that Ayodhya continues to be governed by a capable and experienced leader after my departure. In my opinion, you are the most qualified for this role," Ram replied.

"But after you, Kush is the rightful heir to Ayodhya," Bharat countered.

"Kush is still immature.

(He spent some time in Dakshina Koshal and later established his capital at Kushavati, while Luv founded Shravasti as his capital.

This is now located in the Gonda or Bahraich district. The city of Luvpur in Punjab was named after Luv and is presently known as Lahore. Shrutayudha, the last king of Kush's lineage, and Brihaddal from Luv's lineage participated in the MahaBharat war. Luv's dynasty continued, with

Prasenjit being a notable figure from that lineage, which is also referenced in the history of Buddha's era.)

"I wish to emphasize that I seek to be relieved from the responsibilities of governance," Ram added.

"Brother, with your guidance, Kush will manage the kingdom of Ayodhya effectively; he is both intelligent and courageous," Bharat asserted.

Ram chose not to respond to Bharat's remark, as he did not wish to disclose his intention to depart from this world. The discussion persisted for a while, after which Kush was unanimously appointed as the successor to Ayodhya.

Subsequently, Kush and Luv were summoned and informed of their new duties.

There ought to have been grand celebrations upon Kush being named the successor of Ayodhya; however, Ram was reminded of his own past when, after being decleared as heir of Ayodhya by his father Dasharatha. He was unexpectedly asked to retreat to the forest. He recalled Sita's plea for him to accompany her and those full of ups and downs moments of his indecision.

Ram deemed it inappropriate to prolong the situation any further and resolved to depart promptly. To prevent any unfavorable circumstances from arising before Kush, he made a decision and addressed Maharishi Vashishtha, stating-

"Rishivar, you are our family priest. The entire assembly is present here. It would have been good if Kush received your blessings regarding the succession to the kingdom of Ayodhya right now."

Ever since the arrival of Atibal's messenger, Maharishi Vashishtha was very apprehensive about the future of Ayodhya. Then Lakshman's departure like this and now Ram's hurrying up in this manner, Vashishtha's apprehensions became stronger.

"Right now?" he asked in surprise.

"Yes, the grand ceremony will be held later," Ram said.

"Okay," saying this Vashishtha called for some materials and reciting mantras and applying tilak on Kush, completed the coronation ceremony in a very brief manner. All the people present there congratulated Kush and after this, the assembly dispersed. Everyone accompanied Vashishtha to the palace door to see him off.

xxxxxxx

After parting ways with Maharishi Vashishtha, the others also took their leave as well, but Bharat and Shatrughan chose to stay with Ram. Following this event Ram went into his chamber, settled down and asked for his brothers to join him. As soon as Bharat took his seat, he cast a glance at Ram, seemingly eager to speak but Ram took the lead in the conversation.

"Bharat, it appears you have something on your mind," he said with a light chuckle.

"Yes, it is so," Bharat replied.

"Please say what you want to, don't hesitate."

"I am curious to know your reason for departing from the kingdom."

"Bharat, it is not just this kingdom; I must relinquish everything that is not mine. In fact, the term 'leave' is not perfect, as leaving can bring about suffering. Therefore, it is not a matter of leaving; it is to attain freedom from these. Liberation does not carry the sorrow associated with leaving; rather, it brings joy."

"You said that we have to be free from everything."

"Yes, from everything."

"What did it mean?" Bharat asked.

"Everything means everything. What is mine, Bharat?"

Bharat was taken aback by Ram's response, and concern etched itself on his face.

"What do you consider not yours?" Bharat pressed.

"What is truly mine? Not even this body."

"Are you contemplating abandoning it as well?"

"Language alters meanings, Bharat. I do not wish to relinquish anything; however, freedom is the most valuable pursuit, even from this body, which is not mine. We should seek liberation from it as well."

"Will this talk of liberation from the body not be unfair to us and is the grief of Lakshman's departure the reason for this sudden decision?" said Bharat.

"There are many questions hidden in your question, Bharat. I cannot even think of being unfair to anyone, and my decision is not impulsive. This thought had arose even before Lakshman's passing. His departure has only fortified it.

Bharat, do not mourn Lakshman's absence; there exists a state beyond sorrow and joy. It is a state devoid of craving, condemnation, boredom, praise, violence, non-violence, arrogance, humility, compassion, surprise, anger, enjoyment, or aversion. I have no longing for salvation even. Additionally, there is something more than sorrow of Lakshman's departure."

"And what is that?" Bharat inquired.

"If desires persist while breath ceases, it results in death. Conversely, if desires vanish while breath continues, it leads to liberation, irrespective of whether breath still remains thereafter. Based on my understanding of Lakshman and Sita, I can assert that they have not died in that sense."

Bharat acknowledged, "Yes, it is so," and after a brief pause, he asked, "And what about the message from Maharishi Atibal?"

"The content of that message was already present in my thoughts," Ram responded,

Bharat then posed another question, "Is this sacrifice of the body not parallel to suicide? Whether suicide is ever justified?"

Ram fell silent for a moment before replying,

"After all that I have said, does this question still persist? I am not this body, Bharat and I do not assert this merely for the sake of argument. My journey is not towards renouncing the body but towards attaining liberation from it."

Bharat asked, "What distinguishes the renunciation of the body from liberation from it?"

"Renouncing the body liberates one from the experiences associated with it, yet it does not eliminate the feelings of the body. When bodily pain becomes intolerable, death may feel like liberation; however, the realization that there is no distinction between oneself and God draws one closer to divine understanding. This realization is the initial step towards liberation, and the conviction of unity with God fosters a lasting sense of divine awareness. This is true freedom from the body."

Bharat and Shatrughan found themselves unable to pose further questions on this topic, yet their inquiries lingered in their minds. Ram perceived their unvoiced concerns and remarked, "The domain of questions and answers is boundless, but there is something beyond that. Questions may arise regarding my actions too," he continued.

"Then," Bharat prompted.

"There is no limit to questions and answers, but there is something beyond questions and answers and questions would be raised on me only when I will be going to do something.'' he said.

"What does it mean?'' said Bharat.

"I am not planning to take any specific action, yet in this expansive universe, events unfold continuously. Just as questions and answers are limitless, so too is knowledge. When one realizes that there is no separation between oneself and the universe, and begins to understand the concepts of Soaham, Shivoaham, or Aham Brahmasmi i.e. 'I am that very person,I am Shiv. I am the pure consciousness. Then everything else loses significance. After this, there is neither acceptance nor rejection, because this vastness neither accepts nor rejects anything.

After a brief pause, Ram addressed Bharat, saying,

"Bharat, look at me."

Bharat looked at him.

"Bharat, I am free from all faults, unblemished, peaceful and beyond nature. I am the knowledge and light. This world is illuminated by me. I cannot be destroyed. I do not come or go anywhere but am everywhere and the wonder is that this whole world is from me but does not affect me.

Bharat, the one who knows everything and is the bliss personified, I am the completeness and I am the only one who is complete.

After the argument is over, I am the only one left and the search for the last possible solution ends with me." Saying this, Ram got up and started walking towards the door of the room. Bharat and Shatrughna also got up.

"We want to follow you," Bharat said.

"I do not stop you, you are free to choose your path and it can also be following someone else, but Bharat, following anyone can be meaningful only up to a certain extent. Its result will also be limited. To be limitless, one has to achieve it by erasing the self.''

Bharat and Shatrughna silently listened to Ram and said nothing, but after saying this Ram started walking again.

He came out of the room, came to the door of the building, crossed it turned back, touched the door threshold, bowed, and then started walking again. When the security personnel came to accompany him, Ram stopped them,

"There is no need for you to come with me." He said to security personnel and then walked towards Saryu with a completely detached expression. There was nothing like excitement, remorse, sorrow, despair, or pain in him. His mind was calm and free of emotions.

Bharat and Shatrughan trailed closely behind him. None was looking back. Upon reaching the riverbank, Ram halted, stood still, and observed the flowing water. Memories of Lakshman surfaced in his mind, and he envisioned his face vividly.

Closing his eyes, he seemed to seek to imprint Lakshman's image within his memory.

After a few moments, he opened his eyes and started looking in the oppoSeete direction of the flow of water. There was an open sky as far as the eye could see and the silver sheet of the river.

'Where is it coming from?' Ram thought while looking at Sarayu, turned his head a little backward, looked at Bharat and Shatrughna, and said,

'The Himalayas are this side, right?'

Though both of them were looking calm, but somewhere inside they were filled with various kinds of thoughts. Dispassion was taking birth in their minds, but at the same time there was a fear of some big misfortune. This question of Ram broke the silence spread all around. They were a little startled, but at the same time it felt as if they have found a lead or direction.

"Yes", replied Bharat briefly. Ram heard Bharat's "yes", then looked towards Ayodhya. For a moment, the whole family came in front of his eyes. Sita too. His lips tilted a little, tightened slightly and then a slight smile came. He looked towards the origin of Saryu and then started walking in that direction as if by himself.

Bharat and Shatrughna were still behind him.

Some waves arose in the flowing water of Saryu and disappeared after going some distance.

Some birds sitting on a tree flew and got lost somewhere in the sky.

xxxxxxx

Like other inhabitants of Ayodhya, Manas and Chitra were also sad and dejected. They were tired of weeping.

"Chitra."

"Yes."

"You were right. Ram who had suffered a great loss will not be able to bear it."

"It was my guess."

"You were right. Where will he be, Chitra? People saw him only till the bank of Saryu, that's all."

"I think, to bring him, the gods themselves must have sent a chariot from heaven," said Chitra. Then as if she remembered something, she got up, placed Ram's picture along with Sita's picture in her prayer room, folded her hands, and then both Manas and Chitra bowed down in salutation.

A life
Which was like
Walking on the edge of a sword
In absolute meditation
And then to depart
With absolute neutrality
No wonder
If remembered for ages

Appendix

In the discourse surrounding the cultural heritage of this nation, which spans across epochs, certain individuals cast doubt on the existence of Ram, conveniently overlooking the fact that as one goes deeper into ancient history, the availability of evidence regarding such events diminishes. This phenomenon persists. Not only did C. Gopalachari, the first Governor General of independent India, regard the Ramyana as a historical document, but numerous foreign scholars have echoed this sentiment. Among them is the Indologist Sir William Jones, who conducted extensive research on South Asia. Other notable scholars who have explored the civilization and history of the Ramyana era include Philip Luzendorff from the University of California, Joe Burkhalter and Laurie Sears from the University of Michigan, and B.W.L. Smith from Stockholm University.

Numerous locations in India, Nepal, and Sri Lanka are linked to the events of the Ramyana. While archaeological evidence for these Seetes remains elusive, it is noteworthy that similar evidence for the founders of Christianity and Islam is also lacking. Critics who challenge the supernatural elements described in the Ramyana do not extend the same scrutiny to the miraculous occurrences accepted in other faiths.

Research into the Ramyana has revealed its remarkable geographical accuracy. Many Seetes along Ram's journey into the forest are identifiable and are associated with ancient traditions. It is important to recognize that thousands of years ago, the resources available to a writer were insufficient to facilitate visits to these locations, study local customs, or construct temples to validate their narratives.

Ram was born in Ayodhya and married in Mithila, Nepal. There is Janaki-Kund near Mithila which people believe to have been built by King Janak and have reverence for it. After marriage, Ram and Sita came to Ayodhya from Mithala via Lumbini. There is a pillar built by Emperor Ashoka in Lumbini on which there is mention of the visit of Lord Ram and Gautam Buddha there.

Dandak forest, where most of the time of Lord Ram's exile was spent, was spread over present-day Madhya Pradesh, Chhattisgarh, Orissa, and Andhra Pradesh.

An interesting fact is that a few years ago, two botanists from Chennai travelled the route of Ram from Ayodhya to Lanka to verify the authenticity of the description of the plants coming on Ram's path in Valmiki's Ramyana. He completed this journey by spending three years studying the vegetation on the way.

While talking to 'The Pioneer' newspaper after this visit, Amirthalingam said-

"We followed the path of Lord Ram, Sita, and Lakshman from Ayodhya to Lanka. Surprisingly, almost all the plants and animals mentioned in Valmiki Ramyana were found at the places described in them.

Taxonomists (knowledgeable about the theory of classification of plants and animals) confirmed this from their Sanskrit and Latin names.

According to Nandita Krishnan, supervisor of this research project and director of CPR environmental Education

"Valmiki knew the vegetation, animals, and geographical conditions of this route very well. We found the plants and animals which were described in the Ramyana at those places.

This study revealed that Valmiki was fully aware of the natural conditions, geographical conditions, and environment of these places.

This exploratory study conducted by Amritalingam and Sudhakar is published in a book titled 'Animal Diversity In Valmiki Ramyan'

It is noteworthy that even today the Ramyana is represented in various forms across the different nations.

In Leningrad, Russia, numerous texts containing stories from the Ramyana are available in both Russian and Mongolian. The book 'Academy and Sciences' by Professor C.F. Glostun includes several narratives that are popular along the banks of the Volga River in Siberia, among which the Ramyana stories are featured. Additionally, various adaptations of the Ramyana can be found in the libraries of the Kalmyk state in Russia.

Archaeological excavations of the Astrocan civilization in Italy have uncovered numerous houses adorned with wall paintings dating back to 700 BC. These artworks depict two men wielding bows and arrows alongside figures with tails and a woman. The Astrocan civilization once occupied nearly three-fourths of Italy, and the name of Italy's capital, Rome, bears a striking resemblance to the name Ram.

References to Ram are also present in Chinese literature. A text from 742 AD recounts Dasharatha's anguish during Ram's exile, while the work 'Kapi' by 'His-Yi-Chi' from 1600 AD mentions Hanuman. Furthermore, the Chinese version of the Buddhist scripture 'Tripatik' contains two compositions related to the Ramyana, titled 'Anamakam Jatakam' and 'Dasaratha Kathanam'.

According to Father Kamil Bulke, 'Kang-Tseng-Hui' translated 'Anamakam Jatakam' into Chinese in the third century. This translation found in the book 'Lieu - Tutsi - King', although the original text of 'Anamakam Jatakam' is currently unavailable. The narrative does not specify any names but clearly indicates several significant events from the Ramyana, though with evident influences from Buddhism.

According to 'Dasaratha Kathanam', King Dasharatha ruled over Jambu Island. In this narrative, Ram is referred to as Lomo, while Lakshman is called Loman. Loman possesses the strength and skill of Naloyen (Narayan) along with supernatural abilities known as 'Sen' and 'Ra'. Bharat is identified as Poloro, and Shatrughan retains the same name.

Although this tale does not contain numerous events from the Ramyana, it bears a striking resemblance to it. Key elements include the king's infatuation for the queen, his vow to her, the queen's disinterest in Lomo's throne, her request for the kingdom for her son Poloro, and the subsequent exile of Lomo. The narrative also tells about the king's demise, Poloro's sojourn in a foreign land, his refusal to ascend the throne upon his return, his mother's opposition, and his efforts to persuade Lomo to return from the forest. Ultimately, Lomo is reinstated on the throne, and the kingdom is handed over to him upon his return.

In Buddhism, the 'Dasaratha Jataka', composed around 200 BC, also refers Ram and Sita. Although their significance has been notably reduced in this context, their existence remains acknowledged. Jain literature features contributions from Vimala Suri, Sanghadasa, and Gunabhadra regarding the Ram story. Additionally, comprehensive discussions on the Ramyana and its characters can be found in works such as Ravi Sen's Padmapuran, Swayambhu's Pamachariyu, Harisen's Katha Kosh, and Pushpadant's Mahapuran.

Hanuman is also mentioned in Jain texts, where his mother is named Anjana and his father is Pavanjay. The accounts of Hanuman's birth and upbringing differ somewhat from other traditions. Jain scriptures classify Ram as one of the 63 notable Shalaka men, among whom are nine incarnations of Balabhadra, Narayan, and Pratinarayan. Ram is identified as the eighth Balabhadra, while Lakshman and Ravan are recognized as the eighth Narayan and Pratinarayan, respectively.

In Jainism, the figures of Ram, Lakshman, and Ravan are referred to as Baldev, Vasudev, and Prativasudev, respectively. A notable distinction in the Jain narrative is that Lakshman, rather than Ram, was responsible for Ravan's death, as Ram is depicted as non-violent who later renounces worldly life to become a Jain monk, ultimately achieving the salvation. Additionally, it is stated that Lakshman inadvertently killed Shambuk.

The Pushpadant Mahapuran also references Balram and Krishna, indicating that Krishna was not only a contemporary of the twenty-second Tirthankara, Nemi, but also his cousin. This text provides an account of the MahaBharat, concluding that the Pandavas, like Nemi, ultimately embraced asceticism and attained Nirvana.

According to the Jain scripture Padmapuran, Ram is identified as Padma. Sanghadasa foretold that Mandodari's firstborn would bring about the downfall of Ravan's lineage. This child was Sita, whom Ravan attempted to have killed by entrusting her to his uncle at birth. However, the uncle instead delivered her to King Janak of Mithila, informing him that she was found in the furrows of his plough. Consequently, Janak and his wife, Dharini, became Sita's adoptive parents.

Lord Ram is believed to be a descendant of Ichchhavaku, with the Pali equivalent of this name being Okkaka. The Shakya lineage of Gautam Buddha traces back to Okkaka, which also includes Mandhata and King Sagar. The Ichchhavaku dynasty, recognized as the Surya dynasty, is of significant importance in Jainism, as twenty-two out of the twenty-four Tirthankaras belong to this lineage.

Thailand is primarily a Buddhist nation; however, the Ramyana, referred to as Ramkin, holds significant cultural importance within the country. The Wat Phra Kaew, or the Green Buddha Temple, is regarded as the most esteemed pilgrimage Seete for Buddhists. Located in Bangkok, adjacent to the royal palace, this temple features a green Buddha idol. The temple complex encompasses over a hundred structures and is enclosed by a wall approximately two kilometers in length. Notably, the entire wall is adorned with high-quality paintings depicting the Ramyana, executed with exceptional artistry, colour, and craftsmanship. These murals are divided into 178 sections and are restored every few decades.

In various South Asian nations, Hanuman has long been celebrated as a valiant and dynamic hero. In Thai boxing, several striking techniques bear names linked to Hanuman. The reigning king of Thailand is officially known as Rajaram (the ninth).

Indonesia, while home to a significant Muslim population, showcases the Ramyana through traditional shadow puppetry, which enjoys widespread popularity. In the Philippines, the renowned Sinkil dance is inspired by the narrative of Ram. The ancient islands of the Philippines feature a local depiction of the Ramyana, known as 'Maharadiya Lavan.' Certain Muslim communities in the region maintain a connection to the Ramyana, with numerous tales derived from it being well-received among the 'Marinio' and 'Magandanao or Sulu' Muslims.

Another very surprising thing is that the word 'Ramyana' is found as a surname in the profiles of some people, such as -

Angela Cooky Ramyan (.Dhamsam Gyavapam Ramyan) Aj Ramyan (.R Ramyan) Glory Jolt Ramyan (.L.S. Ramyan) Dennis Ramyan (.K.D.P. Ramyan) etc.

In Malaysia, Ramyan is found in both literary and folklore forms. Here Ramyan is used for social education. Here Ram does not have a religious form. He is established as the ideal of goodness, morality and justice who won over evil due to these qualities.

The Ramyan of the Malay people also reflects their own civilization. Malay writers and narrators give more importance to Lakshman than Ram. According to them, Ram was moral and virtuous but used to stay back and

Lakshman was courageous and reacted decisively. Hence, Malays praise Lakshman more. They call Ram as Ram but Sita as 'Shinto'.

In 1989, the biggest Ram temple was built in Malaysia's northern province Perak near the Thai border which is 250 kilometers away from its capital Kuala Lumpur. It has 1001 idols and paintings.

In Malaysia, the shadow puppet show based on the Ram Katha is very popular for entertainment. All the people who perform it are Muslims, although orthodox Muslims oppose it a lot. They also strongly oppose the music played in it. In this music, the sound produced by the gong orchestra produces the effect of going into a trance.

The association of Indian mind with Ram and Ram Katha is so natural that we can consider it spontaneous but the question is what was so attractive in this story and its characters that Mongolia, Japan, Burma, Laos, Cambodia, Thailand, Indonesia, Philippines etc. many Asian countries have adopted it in some form or the other.

It is to be understood that any imaginary, mythological character cannot reach such a large part of the world and survive for such a long time or get respect.

In Ramyana, Maharishi Valmiki has written in Uttar Kand that in a fierce battle with Vishnu, out of the three sons of demon Sukeshu and Devvati, Malyavan, Sumali and Mali, Mali was killed and Malyavan and Sumali left Lanka and went to live in Paataal. If we try to understand the word 'Paataal', it seems to be around "foot-foot". In the twenty-ninth verse of this session, he writes that Sumali roamed in the netherworld with his family for a long time. This Sumali was the maternal grandfather of Ravana, Vibhishan, Kumbhkaran and Suparnakha.

There is a self-governing region called Somali-land in Somalia, a country in North East Africa and W.H. Press Coat has written a book 'Bhagwatl-Bhut-Namej-Dimagpbv' on Mexico, a country in North America.

In this, he writes that the people of the Aztec (Aztec) community there believe that a beautiful person had come to their country from the east, which was suffering from a natural calamity, who had introduced them to many aspects of progressive civilization. As a result of which, that time was called the golden age of that ancient period, but that person suddenly went back to his country due to some divine reason.

Pressland writes that this is not a folklore but is also available in the form of records. Naturally, the strings of this incident are connected to Indian civilization.

The distance from Lanka to Somalia is 3828 km and from Somalia to Mexico is 15344 km and both Somaliland and Mexico are on the seashore.

Looking at all the above facts, there is a strong possibility that Somali first went to the nearby place Somaliland from Lanka and after living there for some time, due to some reasons, he went to Mexico, which is far away from there and started living there.

Indian philosophy does not differentiate between Ram and Krishna. Ram's area of influence was once very far and Krishna is also acceptable to some religions other than Hindus in some form or the other.

The Jataka tales of Buddhism describe the stories of the previous births of Gautam Buddha and his disciples. In this, Krishna is described as Dhamma Senapati or the chief commander of religion. In this too, Krishna kills Kansa and with the help of his Sudarshan Chakra, he takes over the entire Jambudweep (ancient India).

In Nara, Japan, there is a depiction of Krishna playing the flute in the Great Buddha Hall of the Todai-ji Temple built by Emperor Somu in 752 BC. In the Japanese form of Buddhism, Krishna has been given a place among the gods as a child who is mischievous, lovable and an embodiment of intelligence.

The Baha'i religion considers Krishna to be the manifestation of God or one of the series of prophets. There, Krishna has been given a place equal to Abraham Moses, Zoroaster, Buddha, Muhammad, Jesus Christ and Bahaullah, the founder of the Baha'i religion.

In Ahmadiya Islam too, its founder Mirza Ghulam Ahmed has described Krishna as the prophet of God. He sees Krishna as the one who brings harmony between man and God.

Mirza Ghulam Ahmed has written that Krishna's Murli is actually the divine knowledge given by him. He writes, "As far as I have known Krishna, he was really so great that he cannot be compared with other incarnations. He was the prophet of his time, to whom spiritual knowledge was given by God himself."

Many new religious movements of the 19th century also accept Krishna with respect. Theosophists are prominent among them. They consider Krishna to be the incarnation of Maitreya (the embodiment of ancient knowledge) and a major guru imparting spiritual knowledge to humanity.

Blavatsky founded the Theosophical Society in the 19th century.

There is a surprising similarity between the teachings of Lord Krishna in the Gita and Theosophy. The guiding principle of Theosophy is 'Look inside yourself, there is light, consciousness, knowledge, awareness and God.'

Some so-called intellectual minds may not be satisfied with any evidence and they may not even believe that history is beyond evidence but for those minds which are not prejudiced, the evidences of the existence of Ram and Krishna are scattered everywhere.